My Journey with Food

THE MOST IMPORTANT ELEMENT OF LIFE:
MISTREATED AND MISUNDERSTOOD

Michel Rabu

 FriesenPress

Suite 300 - 990 Fort St
Victoria, BC, Canada, V8V 3K2
www.friesenpress.com

Copyright © 2016 by Michel Rabu
First Edition — 2016

Edited by Leah MacMillan

ISBN
978-1-4602-6349-5 (Paperback)
978-1-4602-6350-1 (eBook)

1. Cooking

Distributed to the trade by The Ingram Book Company

Table of Contents

Preface

Eating is the most important action we do on a daily basis. As a matter of fact, it's one thing that we can't do without. Most ethnic nations consider eating as a time to relax and socialize with family and friends, so time is not a consideration, whether preparing or sitting down to eat. Unfortunately in North America we have not learned to do this yet! Consequently, we look at food as fuel for our body, so fast food…processed food…What is the difference? It's all fuel! Unfortunately this kind of approach has its consequences, all we have to do is look at the statistics on obesity, type 2 diabetes, heart problems and cancer in North America versus other nations. These other nations with lower levels of all of the above generally tend to treat meals as social events, that are relaxed and enjoyable compared to the eat and run we all seem to be consumed by and these nations also have not been exposed to the fast foods, soda, etc.

In my coffee shop I see people come in for lunch with cell phone in hand, busy texting totally disconnected from the food on their plate. No enjoyment or identification of the food they are eating; this behavior cannot be good for the digestive system.

Taking time to relax and eat in a social manner is not a luxury but rather an investment in your health. When you think of two hours a day, half an hour for breakfast, half an hour for lunch, and one hour for dinner, could change you lifestyle and improve your general health. If we don't change our eating habits, the alternative at the rate we are going at today will be a unsustainable healthcare system and more and more young people will be afflicted with completely preventable health issues that will negatively impact our workforce and productivity as a nation.

In The Beginning

La Roche Derrien is a small town in Brittany on the West Coast of France where I grew up during the war years. We lived in a two-storey house made of pink granite with a slate roof, which is the traditional look of homes in Brittany. The town seemed to have been frozen in time since the early 1800's. I don't think anything has changed. Until the early 1950's one still had to go to the local city well daily to get potable water, other water was gathered through a cistern fed by the eaves through.

The church St. Catherine was built in 1447, it still has beaten earth for a floor and wooden chairs with thatched straw seats. A stained glass wall rises thirty feet or more behind the altar, depicting the battle of 1347 where Charles de Blois was killed fighting the English. The altar is hand carved solid oak with intricate designs and at the back of the church there is a huge pipe organ that originally came from Westminster Abbey in London. The building is typical "Gothic" architecture with great acoustics. Outside, all around the perimeter of the church was the original cemetery, which through the ages due to erosion and rain many human bones have surfaced, so eventually all remains were transferred to a new modern cemetery just outside of town. The church along with the city hall are the main buildings in town.

The rest of La Roche Derrien is a cluster of two-storey homes welded together all starting from "Place de la Mairie". Better known as the City Square, "Place de la Mairie", is where all major community events take place, including a weekly fresh produce market which represents local farmers and fisherman. All of the important stores are located around this square. Buildings in La Roche Derrien are made of local pink granite blocks that are two feet thick, the roofs are made of hand cut slate tiles or thatched straw. This style of Breton building is still practiced to this day and is controlled by the building code to ensure the continuing Breton style is not lost.

The "Bretons" are a tough breed of people who still have to this day their own living language "Brezhoneg"; it's a Gaelic dialect similar to Cornish and Welsh (who immigrated to Brittany between the 3rd and 9th century which at that time was known as the "Armorican" peninsula). The "Bretons" also have their own "National" anthem "BRO GOZH MA ZADOU" which is taught in schools. Traditional costumes are worn on special occasions; most of the costumes include a puffy sleeved shirt, with a vest over it, made of embroidered velour. Women wear a "coiffe" on their head, which is a heavily starched lace bonnet; the style of the bonnet differs depending on what region of Brittany you are from. Everyone wears "sabots" which are hand carved wooden clogs with straw inside which is changed daily; women's "sabots" are made up of a wooden sole and leather upper straps which make them much lighter to wear. Another inheritance from our Celtic cousins is the "Biniou" which is a single stem bagpipe; it is similar in tone to the "Scottish" version, but with greater variety in tone selection and not as whiny as the Scottish version. The "Biniou" is the Breton instrument of choice played at all public events.

Brittany is also known as the breadbasket of France. Most of the Brittany's land is used for food production and the coast for aquaculture, which supplies most of the fresh seafood for the Paris market.

I must say my years spent in La Roche Derrien were good years, although we didn't have much. I can remember waking to the smell of fresh baked bread coming from the wood fired oven of the local bakery as if it were yesterday. It's amazing how we can retain smell & taste experiences for such a long time, in my case over 60 years.

During the war my mother worked in a bomb factory making grenades, while my father was drafted into the army at age 19. He was a dispatch rider; his job was to deliver operational documents from HQ to the front lines. He rode a motorcycle with a sidecar, a FN machine gun strapped around his

(A typical traditional Brittany celebration, circa 1920)

neck and he was off! He was captured by the German forces in Normandy and sent to a prisoner of war camp somewhere north of Poland; he managed to escape, but was re-captured and sent to another camp, where he escaped once more. He was now a much wanted man so he joined the "Maquis", a French underground movement specializing in sabotage by blowing up bridges, telegraph poles, railway tracks, setting booby traps, anything that would disrupt German activities in the area. Having escaped from two German prisoner of war camps the Germans were rather anxious to re-capture him. My father later learnt that he was a "shoot on site person" so his activities were all nocturnal and he would come to see us once or twice a month when possible. I was five years old before I had my father at home with us on a daily basis.

Staying at my Grandmother's farm during the war was the most logical and safest solution, since the Germans were still around, and food was more readily available as we grew as much as possible at the farm. Even though we never had a surplus, the Germans would come on a regular basis to requisition food for the troops, so we had to hide as much as we could for our family and ourselves. The best vegetables to store were potatoes, leeks, turnips, parsnips, rutabagas, carrots as well as apples and pears from the orchard. At an early age I was obliged to like root vegetables for there was not much other choice. We were also lucky to have a few chickens, a couple of pigs and a few cows. This meant my grandmother would always have a slab of pork hanging in the chimney, smoking away and some days she would cut a piece of smoked pork, mainly fat mind you but it was protein. The odd hen that would stop laying eggs ended-up the same way; she would boil it with all available root vegetables and we would have a feast along with fresh baked bread, baked in that wood fired oven, made with coarse ground, locally milled whole wheat flour. Traditionally the typical Brittany bread weighed about one kilo, and is round with a thick crust dusted with flour and made daily. The next day leftover bread would be sliced into chunks and served on top of soup, which often became our meal for the day, simple but healthy and good.

Fresh churned, unsalted butter was made every four or five days from the fresh cream from our farm. My job was to turn that seemingly huge handle on the wooden, barrel shaped churner; I seemed to take hours and often I had to call my grandmother to take over. Once you heard the sloshing of the buttermilk you knew that the butter was ready, then you saved the but-termilk to drink and put the big mound of butter on a tea towel to absorb the excess moisture. I remember the butter had a fresh picked hazelnut fragrance to it, sweet and soft, no salt was added so the shelf life was three days at most, as there were no fridges to be had in those days during the war. The kitchens in farmhouses in Brittany are very big; they are designed to accommodate groups of up to ten or twelve temporary farm workers at a long communal table with benches for seats. There is always a huge floor to ceiling fireplace where one could cook a whole pig. This is also where the traditional "Crémaillière" would hang, which is a cast iron cauldron pot that is hung on a pivotal frame. The pivotal frame allows you to position the cauldron close to the fire or away from the flame depending what you were cooking; soup or stew, there was always something simmering in that huge pot!

On the other side of the kitchen from the long table were three or four "lits-clos"; these are recessed beds in the wall, used to accommodate visitors or casual workers, this is where I slept. The mattresses of these beds were made at the farm after the harvest; two large linen sheets were sewn together and stuffed full of fresh harvested oat husks. These mattresses would be about a meter thick and when you jumped into them you would sink down and the fresh smell of oats would permeate the whole room along with the smell of burning oak wood in the fireplace that would burn all night.

It's amazing how little things from your youth stay with you with such clarity and bring joy all over again. My school friends' Father was the local baker and during the summer holidays I would spend time helping at the bakery. I was ten years old then and wouldn't get paid but in return he would give me a couple loaves of bread or croissants. Now we are talking about a real bakery here! Bundles of firewood would be delivered by horse cart on a regular basis in order to feed the oven. The dough mixing machine was a mechanical manual unit with a large crank handle that I could barely move. My job was to put the dough in racks lined with canvas to proof before baking and also to put the bread on the shelves for sale later that morning. I forgot to tell you, I started to work at midnight and the first customers came at 7am to pick up their bread and other baked goodies, for in France you buy your bread daily; I guess that's where the phrase "give us our daily bread" came from! French people like their food fresh, most have a very small fridge compared to North American standards and that is because of two reasons: First, electricity is very expensive and second, going out daily to the market assures you of freshness and allows you to socialize with the people. This is part of the French culture, a way of know what's going on. I know we have social media now… sorry, it's not the same.

In France, unless you are in a large city, food chain stores such as we are accustomed to do not exist nor do they succeed. People want fresh, local products. They want to meet the producer, and have a social interaction at the same time, now try that at your local super market! Because of this, it's very rare that you get bad meat, fish or anything. The producer knows you'll be around again tomorrow or the next day and the last thing he wants is to hear you scream at him because the fish was not quite fresh enough or the lamb chops were tough, or the vegetables had some rot or were bruised. After all his reputation at that market is at stake and everyone will hear about the fracas you created, he may as well move to another province. Now just think, wouldn't you want that kind of relationship with your food supplier!

Here in North America, instead we have the "we'll give you a credit or refund attitude" but as far as I am concerned it's too late mate! The damage is done I cannot trust you again. Also think of the benefits of shopping with local producers: carbon footprint lowered, food security controlled, freshness assured, money benefits the local economy and jobs are created; these reasons alone should make you want to change the way you shop. I know what you are thinking, convenience and time. Well maybe it's time to slow down and take the time to smell the coffee and get back to enjoying the real treasures of life. Otherwise you won't have the memories to recall later on in life when you now have the time. Sure, you'll recall the hustle and bustle of Friday night shopping, a cart full of processed foods, a line up at the cashier, a store that couldn't care less if you came back or not, nor about the food they sell you, that is full of chemicals that most likely will harm you and your family.

Today we don't take food seriously enough. It is all about convenience. If we looked around us we can see the disastrous effect it's having on our youth and society in general, obesity, diabetes, high blood pressure, vascular problems, etc. All of this will create a serious strain on our health care system and national productivity. We need to re-evaluate food, what we eat, where it's grown, how it's grown. This will only change if we change our attitude about food. Maybe the French saying is now more important than ever before… "The British eat to live, the French live to eat" (and drink I may also add).

This book is going to analyze the pros and cons of food production, its effect on our society and those that produce it, the health benefits and consequences of poor nutrition on the individual and our health care system, along with guidelines to better health and the joy and satisfaction of cooking. Keeping in mind to "keep it simple".

"Be the change you want to see in the world"
Mahatma Gandhi

Where Do We Start?
With Shopping

Let's start with shopping, because this where it all begins. You may have to break a few bad habits that are responsible for the way you eat and feel, remember you also are responsible for the health of your family. Growing children don't understand the difference between "good food" and "bad food". Taste is acquired through repetitive exposure to various types of food; you are not born hating broccoli. Granted some foods are more palatable than others and we all have our favorites, but a child that has never tasted a "Big Mac" or a "Coke" will never miss it! So early conditioning to good healthy food is the responsible task for parents to practice; don't blame your kids for eating junk food. We teach our kids so many skills whilst they are growing up, but the skill that will affect their lives the most we ignore! Eating healthy. So this is where we must start.

Some rules about shopping for food: NEVER shop when you are hungry, because this is when you are most vulnerable to being attracted to food that are high in fat, sugar, and fancy packaging. The eyes in your hungry stomach are doing the buying, don't go there! If you do as a rule you'll end up buying processed food that your hungry stomach remembers from TV or store advertising. When you are hungry you are very vulnerable to impulse buying; you want food in your stomach and you don't want to spend time cooking. You want it NOW! No fuss, no muss! And that's when you end-up with a cart full of processed food.

The best way to start is by planning your menu ahead for the next few days and making a list of the items that you'll require; this allows you to think smart when shopping. Think if I want chicken breast for one meal, why don't I buy a whole chicken? You can cut the breast out, do the same with the thighs, save the wings in the freezer so that when you have enough of them you can have a wing night! Do the same with the tenders, again when you have a few saved you can use them to make a chicken stir-fry. Also save the bones in the freezer to make chicken stock. Cutting a chicken is not rocket science, and I'll show you how further on. Now you have three meals ready when you want them, plus the best chicken stock you can buy and in the process you have saved a lot of money. Unlike commercial chicken stocks, which have ingredients that you cannot pronounce and most likely 20-30% sodium and maybe if you're lucky some chicken fat, your stock on the other hand will taste like chicken stock should. If you wish you can omit the sodium completely and you certainly won't have any chemicals or additives that are harmful to your health.

When shopping buy your proteins first, fish, meat and chicken. Pay attention to the price per kilo, for instance chicken thighs with skin ON verses chicken thighs with skin OFF, you will be surprised at just how much you are paying for someone to peel back the skin. You could be doing this yourself and saving the skins for making a chicken stock down the road. Just put the skins in the freezer along with your vegetable trimmings until you have enough to make a batch. Now, you'll have a healthy stock at a price you can afford, low in SODIUM content if you choose, and no added chemicals or preservatives. You will be amazed at the flavour of your stock, as well as your savings at the end of the month.

The same process can be used with, fish, other meats and vegetables. For example with pork, when I am making spare ribs I always boil my ribs first for three reasons: first to remove as much fat as I can, two to tenderize the meat, and three to make some "pork stock". In a large pot put enough water to cover the ribs and a little more, add one sliced onion, 2 tablespoons of soya (for every kilo of meat), one tablespoon of sesame oil, and one table-spoon of ginger. Bring to a slow boil for about twenty minutes then remove the ribs and brush on a marinade on both sides; the ribs are ready to bake in the oven or on the BBQ (See the Spices and Rub Mixes section for a great marinade recipe). Now strain the stock and refrigerate overnight. The next day you'll see a white film on the surface, skim that film off, it is all fat; we don't want nor do we need it. Now you have a wonderful wonton soup base.

To create the best tasting wonton soup all you have to do is bring the stock to a boil, add sliced mushrooms, chopped green onions, sliced broccoli, and/ or bok choy, shrimp, and wontons (Asian food stores have them and are usually very good). Boil for 3-4 minutes only, you want your vegetables to be crunchy and fresh tasting. Top with a little soya sauce and there you have it. Now that was easy and cheap to make, and as a bonus it is healthy. You can also freeze your stock for use at a later time. This stock can be used when making a stir-fry, or chow mein.

So you see it's not complicated all you need is your imagination to take over, be creative and above all "keep it simple" don't let cooking become a chore or boring make it a creative unique experience for all to enjoy. Your reward will come from your family or guests, who are amazed at your new creative cooking skills, not to mention the money you will save and you'll keep your family healthy.

Here are simple guidelines I follow when buying my meat.

CHICKEN:

Buy whole ones, so that you can make stock with the trimmings. This also gives you chicken breasts at half the price of prepackaged ones, same goes for drumsticks, and thighs.

PORK:

Is misconstrued when it comes to healthy meats, but if you buy the proper cuts it's actually very lean. I recommend whole pork loins, just trim the fat and derive a variety of cuts from that one loin and you save a lot of money.

BEEF:

I am rather selective, because I don't want to eat too much beef, so we will work with some good valued and lean cuts. Two cuts that I prefer for both quality and value are sirloin strip for steaks and tenderloin if I want to do a dinner party and impress my guests.

FISH:

Controversy, do we use wild or do we use farmed salmon? That is the question. I prefer wild, of course, but I am not going to deprive myself of fresh salmon just because the season is closed. The quality of the waters where salmon is farmed in Canada is pristine, the feed the fish receive has in the past being questionable but new regulations have improved the situation. What I stay away from are fish and shrimp from Asia. These fish and shrimp are mainly raised in shallow ponds in a tropical climate where hygiene is not a mandatory factor, nor are there any controls on the type of feed. A word of caution: shrimp that have not being properly de-veined are apt to carry many varieties of unwanted diseases causing bacteria so if using Asian farm raised shrimp make sure the vein is totally removed and rinse the shrimp well before cooking. For me, here on the West Coast, local shrimp and prawns are the only option; the quality and taste is unequaled, sure you are going to pay a little more for the product but it's well worth it.

LAMB:

Fresh local lamb is always best and the most popular cuts are the leg and racks (which I'll give you recipes for again simple and great tasting). Frozen New Zealand is an excellent substitute for fresh, it's all in the preparation. I prefer New Zealand lamb products, to Australian, reason being NZ lamb is usually younger, so less fat, more tender and a milder smell.

Now back to shopping, the next aisle you want to go to after protein selection is vegetables and fruits. This is a difficult area in the store to be in because you are bombarded with colors, variety, and some smells if you're lucky. Most of the time, the fruits are from exotic places and have been picked green to allow for the long transportation, so by the time we get them although they look good, there's no flavour. So the lesson to learn is NOT to buy fruits that are out of season. First you'll avoid disappointment and second you'll save a lot of money. I know when you see cherries, for example, in December from Chile, you think summer, sun, fun, but what you usually get is hard, tart, and a flavour that if you were blindfolded you wouldn't be able to tell what you were even eating! So, why go there? Wait for your local fruits to come into season and you'll enjoy the true flavour of the fruits and you'll be helping the local economy.

When choosing fresh vegetables the key word is FRESH. Don't just grab off the shelf; take a close look to see if it's ripe, firm, no bruises, no rotten spots, not wilted. After all you are paying for quality, so why settle for less? So often I see people just grab vegetables or fruits without even looking at them and then they wonder why they don't last more than a day in the fridge.

Root vegetables, you usually don't see much action in that section of the store except for older people who know the value and benefits of these vegetables. I have included recipes further on for root vegetables that will have your family asking for more. Simple, tasty and good for your health and pound for pound you get the best value as well.

So often we hear the excuse "I buy frozen or canned because I don't have the time and it's easy"; I am sorry but I can't buy that argument. You can prepare a stir fry of fresh healthy vegetables in the same time, and it's not rocket science. First you must have a "wok" the rest is simple. Just a little canola oil in the wok at a high temperature, put in the selected vegetables of your choice, then toss in some of your pork stock and cover and cook for about 4 minutes and done!

Here is a basic combination of vegetables that is sure to please: sliced carrots, sliced mushrooms, peppers pieces, sliced onions, chopped ginger, minced garlic, broccoli and/or cauliflower pieces, baby bok choy, sliced celery. This will give you a variety of texture, color, and flavours that will impress the guests or family and it's healthy and fresh. You can have as many vegetables as you can conjure and as many flavours, all ready in less than 10 minutes. Turn this basic vegetable stir-fry into an Oriental side dish by simply adding a teaspoon of sesame oil and/or soya. The variety is endless; it's all a matter of personal taste choices. The bonus is only one dirty pan to wash!!! Later, I have included a variety of simple tasty recipes for stir-fry.

Now we come to the most confusing department in any food store, cereals and flour. Why do we need 185 varieties of cereal on the shelf? Fancy boxes, bright colors, toys for the kids and as a bonus, lots and lots of SUGAR, FAT, ARTIFICIAL COLOUR, and a bunch of chemicals that no one can pronounce. And for the parents' reward, you get a hyperactive, fat or obese child, but to relieve your guilt you can let your two year old pick the product they like best, so now any dysfunctional side effects can be blamed on the kid! Do yourself a favor, read the nutritional chart on the package before you buy, the simpler the cereal the better, incorporate fresh fruits or dried fruits to enhance the taste and texture if necessary.

The biggest culprit of processed food additives today is HFCS, high fructose corn syrup. This is a cheap substitute for sugar, which in studies has being shown to be responsible for a 20% increase, in type 2 diabetes in children. Do you really want to feed your child anything that contains HFCS? This is why you must read labels.

Flour, the noblest of all cereals, what are they doing to you? For a millennium you have being king, just harvest the wheat, grind it and use it. Why do you need now to be bathed in peroxide or chlorine and other chemicals to make you white, and remove organic vitamins and nutrients? Only then to be replaced with synthetic ones after making you white; am I missing something here in the logic department? I can't ever remember any of my family using white flour. We always use unbleached flour the way it was meant to be, and whenever possible whole wheat is even better. I don't want to WONDER what is in my bread. I'll let our dietician give you all you should know about cereals and nutrition.

A well-stocked pantry is very important plus it can save you a lot of money. I buy canned goods, pasta etc, whenever I see good buys that are on "special". The same applies for foods that can be frozen. With frozen food make sure that there is no air in the packaging before freezing for this will cause freezer burn; I find that most of the time I have to re-pack the products. The biggest problem I find with frozen food is that I keep buying food but if you're like me, you forget to use it. Every month it's best to take a good look at what is in the freezer and rotate the food before it becomes freezer burnt and useless and costly, defeating the reason for the freezer in the first place.

Another way to protect from freezer burn, especially with seafood, is to freeze it in recycled milk containers. Put the fish, oysters, clams, whatever you need to freeze in the container and fill with cold water and freeze; the water will actually protect the food from becoming freezer burnt. I also find this method retains more of the natural flavour of the seafood. The best way of course would be to vacuum pack the food, unfortunately the home units don't seem to work well, and the bags are very expensive to use, and the commercial machines cost a couple of thousand dollars.

Dehydrating is another method of preserving food. I use this method to dry, wild mushrooms, herbs, and fruits during the season. Dehydrating is a great option if you're lucky enough to have local tree ripened fruit available. Don't try with fruit that has little flavour to begin with unless you have a high sugar content in the fruit as you will not achieve a good result, so taste the fruit before deciding if it's good enough to dehydrate. When drying herbs, you don't have to remove the stem before drying, it's a lot easier to do that when the herbs are fully dried. Once dried if you want you can freeze herbs in a plastic bag or jar, this will keep them fresh for a very long time. I like to do that with my fresh basil and thyme, this assures you of the optimum flavour when you use them.

During some of these recipes I'll refer to using butter or cream, my dietician friend would argue with me about the health factor of that, but let's face it, we all have to be bad sometimes, it feels good!!! So it must be good.

Of course I should mention that with all good cooking, spices are the integral element for success. If you purchase your spices in the little 2oz glass jars then you just blew the budget to hell and back. You can buy your spices in the large 16oz jars at most chain food stores; spices keep well so stock up.

Here is a list of the most popular herbs and spices that I would suggest you keep on hand.

- Marjoram
- Thyme, whole, not powder
- Basil, whole
- Sage
- Oregano, whole
- Cumin
- Rosemary, whole
- Curry, paste is good and easy to use, red or green
- Anise, powder
- Star anise whole
- Saffron, Spanish only
  US saffron is not crocus saffron so it is just color and has no flavour
- Paprika, smoked Hungarian is the best
- Chili flakes.
- Italian mix and also a Greek mix
  These mixes are good, and convenient for some general flavour enhancement, they also come in the 16oz size.

Of course there are some herbs that you can grow and dry yourself very successfully, or buy them directly from the farm or at the farmers market, if there is one in your area. Most of these I dry; all you do is harvest them in the fall, tie them in a small bundle and store them upside down them in a cool dry area in an open plastic storage/ freezer bag. You want air to circulate that's why you leave the bag open, otherwise you may develop mold. You could also freeze them whole in a plastic storage/ freezer bag.

Here is a list of those herbs that I grow and use.

- Sage
- Oregano
- Mint
- Parsley
- Chives
- Garlic chives
- Basil
- Dill
- Thyme
- Tarragon
- Rosemary

Another practical way to store fresh herbs is to convert them into compound butter, and this is so simple to do, here is how.

Compound Butter

In a food processor bowl add your selected herb, such as handful of fresh washed basil, and pulse it until it is a puree. Then add 1 cup of butter and 1 cup of NH margarine, scrape the side of the bowl and pulse again a couple of times until you have a smooth buttery mixture. Refrigerate the mixture for 30 minutes or so. Take a piece of plastic film about a foot long, lay it on the counter and spoon the butter mixture on it in the form of a sausage, now gently roll the film and mixture keeping that sausage appearance, tuck both ends in, freeze.

This will keep for as long as you need. Fine, but what do I do with this buttery sausage you ask? Well, let's say you're having a dinner party and for your main you're cooking halibut. How does not really matter, but once cooked you'll take your basil butter, slice it into ½ inch thick pieces and place one on top of each piece of halibut. The butter will melt and add a new flavour dimension to your let's say BBQ halibut.

What we have done with basil, can also be done with, chives, parsley, dill, tarragon, and mint. Let's say you have just cooked some peas, drain the water and drop a couple of slices of mint butter in, stir and now you have buttery mint peas. Dill butter can be used with fish or carrots, tarragon and parsley butter go great with BBQ steaks or chicken, chive & parsley butter go nicely with nugget potatoes, or any type of vegetable, another great compound butter is roasted pepper butter, it will enhance any pasta or vegetable dish. You can also use these butters to put under the skin of the breast of a chicken before roasting it. When you have these compound butters at your disposal, it will change the way you cook and add a new dimension to your food.

Roasted Red Pepper Compound Butter

Ingredients:

4 large red peppers

A few tablespoons of olive oil

1 cup butter

1 cup margarine

Method:

1. Coat peppers with olive oil.

2. Place peppers on a cookie sheet and roast at 400°F until they are black on all sides. You will need to turn them around every few minutes.

3. Once they are nice and black put them immediately in a brown paper bag and seal the end, let them sit for about 20 minutes.

4. Remove them from the bag one at the time, and rinse the dark skin off, under cold water using your fingers to remove all of the skins.

5. Next you want to cut the peppers in half, remove the seeds and the top.

6. Put the peppers in the food processor along with the butter and the margarine. Once your mixture is smooth, proceed with rolling the butter into a sausage shape in plastic film as mentioned before and freeze.

Having these butters at your fingertips will motivate you to experiment with them on different dishes because they are there ready to use. Remember taste is very personal, don't be scared to try different things.

The best way to prepare yourself for this new approach to cooking is what I call "Brain Tasting" this is how it works. When you look at a lemon for example, right away you know what it tastes like. Now you look at a glass of milk and again you acknowledge the taste associated with it. Now imagine mixing the two together and what do you experience? Sour, curdled not what I want to drink. Yet you have not tasted these items yet with your mouth, only your brain is recalling the taste of each and assuming the result of combining both. It's telling you "No it won't work". So when creating a new dish and wanting to know if it'll work or what spice to use, just go through this exercise. Take each spice; remember the taste that is already stored in your brain. Now with practice you'll find that it becomes easy to recognize what works and what doesn't, this is what I call "Brain Tasting".

Here is an example that may surprise you. Imagine this dish combination, penne pasta, chickpeas, spinach, diced tomatoes, basil butter, pine nuts and Parmesan cheese. If you "Brain Taste" all of the above ingredients it tells you that Yes! They will work well together. Try it sometime, it's a great way to get carbs, protein, texture and colour all in one dish, prepared in one pot. So remember if you're not sure whether certain foods or spices will work together do the "Brain Taste". The more brain flavours you can retain, the more versatile your cooking skills will be and the more adventurous you will be about food and spice combinations.

When my son was two years old, he ate, escargots, squid, broccoli…anything you put in front of him. I am talking about serious adult food that I am sure most children wouldn't have even tried, but I always told him try it once, then if you don't like it that's fine, but at least try! And he did, but not before he would smell everything that you put in front of him to eat or drink. To this day 50 years later he still does that, he loves food and wines and has the ability to detect the smallest fragrance in a dish or a wine.

I believe that is a result of "Brain Taste" retention from an early age. We always made sure that our children ate everything that the adults did.

It's all about being responsible; yes, we are accountable to our health care system. Nutrition is the most singular factor in assuring good health, of course aside from genetic pre-disposition of which you have little control. Obesity, diabetes, cardiovascular, hypertension, all can be controlled by a proper diet; that means fresh, natural, balanced, and no super size portion at any time. Diets don't work if you don't change YOUR lifestyle, which is why most people regain their weight after being on a diet for a while. It's all about smaller portions, no snacking, no soft drinks, no processed foods, low sodium intake, and lots of fruits and vegetables and fish. Daily walking after dinner is a good way to exercise and feel better after a meal, and you'll also sleep better and by the way a steady walk is just as good for you as jogging.

Another responsibility that we must practice is sustainability, know where, what, why, by whom, and how your food is produced; encourage local and seasonal buying. When I see acres of crops in perfect rows with no weeds and steroid size growth I ask myself what are they using on my food, do I want to eat it? Remember you are what you eat!

Michel Rabu

Making Your Own Healthy Stocks & Soups

Let's start with some basic recipes that will save you time and money and will be beneficial to your health at the same time. Flavour is best derived from homemade stocks and fresh herbs. You should always have stocks in your freezer, you can freeze them in milk cartons, plastic storage/ freezer bags, or ice cube trays.

The basic stock recipes always incorporate the following ingredients: water, onions, celery, carrots peeled or whole, peppers the colour of your choice, and herbs. I prefer herbes de Provence because it includes all of the basic herbs ready mixed and bay leaf and parsley are also added (See the Spices and Rub Mixes section for the recipe).

Once you have tasted home made stock, you'll never buy stock again, and remember YOU control the sodium , save money and end up with a healthy product. Stocks are the basic elements to most cooking; whether you are making soups, sauces, stews, pasta, or rice, stock will enhance the flavour of all the end products. Rice, for example, cooked in chicken stock rather than water will convince you to never use water again. The Italians use chicken stock when cooking risotto for that very reason. Now if you are planning an Asian theme meal with rice as a side, you may want to use pork stock with a pinch of five-spice, then add chopped green onions on top just before serving, Voilà! Simple and good.

Beef Stock

I like to roast all of my beef bones, fat etc. in a roasting pan with a bottom layer of vegetable trimming that I have saved in the freezer. I add some herbes de Provence and add about 8 cups of water. I'll cook this in the oven at 375°F for about 1 hour, stirring the mixture once or twice, then I'll put all of it into a stockpot along with more water, and slow boil/simmer for about 1 hour. Now bring the beef stock to a full boil, then reduce the heat to a slow simmering boil, covered. Usually I like to cook my stocks for two hours to maximize flavour, after the first hour I'll add four egg whites that I have had frozen (I freeze four to a bag) this is called a raft; a raft coagulates on top, drawing all the fat into it. Let the stock cool overnight, the next day the raft will have hardened and can be easily scooped out in one piece (save it for the compost) now all you have to do is strain, and taste for salt & pepper. All stocks should be strained in a fine mesh colander or cheesecloth. This basic way to make stock can be used when making beef, chicken, pork, or vegetable stocks

If your recipe calls for a strong beef flavour, like for "stroganoff or bourguignon sauce", simply take your basic beef stock and slow cook it until its reduced by half. You may want to add some red wine to your stock prior to reduction (one-third wine to two-thirds stock), this will enhance the flavours. Just before serving this sauce add one tablespoon of butter and whisk it into the sauce, this will make your sauce glossy and add a velvety smoothness.

Our New Home in British Columbia

French Baked Onion Soup

Approximately 12 servings (depending on the size of your bowl)

When my family moved to Vancouver Island in 1972, my father and I opened a restaurant on a beautiful waterfront property between the town of Courtenay, to the south, and the city of Campbell River to the north we called it "The Gourmet by the Sea Restaurant". One of the most popular soups on the menu was French Baked Onion Soup; I used to make at least five gallons a week! I'll share this recipe with you, because of what's involved, I would recommend making this size batch and freezing what you can't use immediately. It will keep in the freezer for months, or in the fridge for at least a week. The best time to serve this soup is on cold wintry night, by the fireplace with a glass of Cabernet Sauvignon, or two.

Ingredients:

24 cups beef stock (dehydrated stock is OK for this recipe)

10 lbs onions (regular yellow)

1 cup Lea & Perrin Worcestershire sauce

1 cup chopped parsley

2 tablespoons black pepper

Salt to taste

2 bay leaves

Canola oil, enough to coat the bottom of the frying pan to fry each batch of onions

1 tablespoon herbes de Provence

1 crouton slice per serving

Shredded Swiss cheese to cover each crouton (2 tablespoons).

Method:

1. Put your beef stock in pot and bring to a simmer boil.

2. Use the largest frying pan you have, (the bigger the less batches you'll have to make) coat the bottom with canola oil and fill halfway with sliced onions.

3. To the onions, add pepper and a pinch of salt, cook, toss or stir over medium heat, until onions are starting to brown (not burn), then add a pinch of herbes de Provence to each batch and a teaspoon of Lea and Perrin. Cook for a couple of minutes more, then transfer cooked onions to the stock. Repeat this method until all onions are used.

4. Add parsley and bay leaf to the stock and slow simmer for 1 hour. Scoop any brown scum that appears on top, the oil from the

cooked onions creates this. At this point, This soup, covered, will keep in the refrigerator for up to five days, but like I said earlier this soup freezes very well, milk quart containers or plastic storage/ freezer bags work well for storage.

5. Reheat stock to serving temperature if required.

6. When serving this soup make some croutons (see below) to put on top before baking.

7. Fill ovenproof bowls ¾ full with the soup, place crouton on top, sprinkle about a tablespoon of shredded cheese, bake until croutons are brown and the soup is bubbling.

Croutons:

1. Sliced bread preferably a rustic multigrain, cut to the size of the bowls you'll be using to bake the onion soup in the oven.

2. Butter the slice (yes, use butter), sprinkle with the shredded Swiss cheese and bake for 5min or so @ 400°F until the bread looks like a melted cheese toast.

Thinking about these soup recipes takes me back to my early childhood in France, after the war, each day I would have to travel by bicycle with my friend Louis to our school some 17 kilometers from home. We had to leave early in the morning to get to school by 8 am. Before leaving home a bowl of coffee with a slice of bread was the regular fare for breakfast in those days, so by lunchtime we were starving. I remember the classroom was cold, especially in the winter, as there was no heat; after all the war had just ended and the government imposed restrictions on all commodities, food, etc. So you went to school with leftover vegetables and meat, if you were lucky enough to have some.

At school you would keep an old can about 16oz in size with a wire handle and the teacher would let you put your can on a potbelly stove, which was in the middle of the classroom. We kept the fire going with wood that we would go out and get every hour or so; now we had some heat and our cans on top would be filled with water and the vegetables and meat we had bought from home. The end result at lunchtime, we had hot soup. As you can see, I have had a very early training when it comes to making soup. I recall my favorite vegetable in those soups was leeks, which my Grandmother grew in her garden; to this day it is still my favorite vegetable which I use whenever possible. I'll give you a recipe for leeks and orange vinaigrette salad further on, a great summer salad.

Imagination is your only limit when it comes to making soups. I'll give a couple more of my favorite soup recipes.

Carrot and Ginger Soup

6 Servings

Ingredients:

5 lbs shredded carrots

2 medium onions diced

4 medium baker potatoes cut into small chunks

1 leek cut into 1" pieces

1 cup diced celery

2 tablespoons fresh grated ginger

1 tablespoon dried ginger

1 teaspoon cumin

12 cups chicken stock

¼ cup canola oil

Salt and pepper to taste

Method:

3. In a 12 quart stockpot add the canola oil and warm for a couple of minutes over medium heat.

1. Add the onions and celery, and let them sweat for about 5 minutes, stirring every few minutes or so.

2. Now add the leeks and do the same.

3. Add your potatoes and carrots, cook and stir for about 5 minutes.

4. Now add your ginger and chicken stock. Stir well and let simmer boil for 1 hour.

5. The next step is easiest if you have a processing stick, also known as a hand blender. Now what you want to do is to process blend all this, it may take five minutes or more to get the soup into a nice smooth textured puree.

6. At this stage I would suggest a taste test, you may want more ginger, a little salt, or some cream to smooth things out, you can substitute the cream with yogurt, your choice. (Freezable)

With any of these soups a drizzle of whole cream in any design and then run a toothpick through your design, eye appeal is very important in food presentation, "if it looks good it must taste good! Sometimes you go out for dinner to a restaurant and everything around you along with the menu looks great, but when the food comes, it just doesn't cut it.

Curried Lentil Soup

6-8 Servings

This next soup we are going to tackle is another of my favorites.

Ingredients:

5 lbs red lentils

4 medium diced onions

1 medium bunch of celery, chopped

4 red peppers, chopped

4-5 medium carrots, diced

½ cup canola oil

4 tablespoons red curry paste

12 cups chicken stock

1 teaspoon cumin

1 quart plain yogurt

Salt to taste

Method:

1. In a 10-12 quart stockpot, heat the canola oil for a minute or two on medium heat.

2. Add the onions, celery, carrots, and peppers, stir all for about 4-5 minutes.

3. Add your curry paste and cumin and stir.

4. Add the chicken stock and bring to the boil, lower the heat to medium and add the lentils. Stir well and bring all to a slow simmer. Cook for about 45 minutes until lentils are soft.

5. With your hand blender, process for about 5 minutes or until you have smooth silky soup with no trace of any vegetables or lentil showing. If you do not have a hand blender, you can use a regular blender, doing small batches at the time and then mixing it all back together in your stockpot. What you are trying to achieve is a smooth cream like consistency to your soup.

6. Before serving add 1 tablespoon full of yogurt in the middle of the bowl and sprinkle finely chopped fresh mint on top. This soup freezes very well.

At the restaurant, we had two dining areas, the classic dining room and the casual "bistro" area. The classic dining room had table linen, fancy crystal glasses, flambées and Caesar salad made at the table and a crew of impeccable waiters. In the front part of the building we had a casual "bistro" offering lighter fare and lighter prices. One day I got fed up seeing all of the trimmings of fresh broccoli going to waste in the garbage, so I decided to make a cream of broccoli soup to serve in the bistro. You have to remember that 30 years ago broccoli was not your favorite vegetable, anyhow 30 years later we still have people drooling over the thought of cream of broccoli soup. How does the saying go? Make it and they'll eat it!!! Well that's my version of the saying and I am sticking to it, so I'll share my recipe for cream of broccoli soup Gourmet by the Sea Restaurant style.

Cream of Broccoli Soup

6 Servings of soup and 16-20 servings of broccoli stock

This recipe will make enough broccoli stock that you'll be able to divide it into four containers to freeze, and each container will yield soup for four-six people.

Ingredients:

BROCCOLI STOCK:

> At least 12 cups broccoli florettes
>
> 8 cups broccoli stems and leaves
>
> 4 medium onions, diced
>
> 1 whole bunch of celery, diced
>
> 2 green peppers, diced
>
> ½ cup canola oil
>
> 1 teaspoon Four Spice (See the Spices and Rub Mixes section for the recipe)
>
> 4 cups chicken stock
>
> 12 cups water

SOUP:

> 1 cup melted margarine
>
> 2 cups warm milk
>
> 8 cups hot broccoli stock
>
> 1 cup flour
>
> 1 cup whipping cream (there I go again) or use half & half if you wish less fat.

Method:

First we make our Broccoli Stock.

1. In a 10-12 quart stockpot, sauté the onions, celery, peppers in the canola oil for about 5 minutes.

2. Add the chicken stock and water, add the four spice and bring to a boil.

3. Add the broccoli florets and stems (I suggest peeling the stems with a potato peeler and cutting them into approximately one-inch pieces). Simmer for about 2 hours with lid on.

4. Using your hand blender, blend all until smooth, then strain through a fine sieve to remove all of the stringy fiber. Now we can make our soup and/or store or freeze broccoli stock for future use.

Soup:

1. Bring eight cups of broccoli stock to a slow boil.

2. In a mixing bowl mix melted margarine with warm milk then add flour and mix until smooth.

3. Whisk mixture into the hot broccoli stock. Bring back to a boil stirring constantly.

4. Add 1 cup of whipping cream*, stir and serve. Bon appétit!

   *If you must, you can substitute the whipping cream with half & half or even skim milk. Now our dietician is happy!

I usually take advantage of early fall when the local farmed tomatoes are just about finished for the year, I'll go to the farm and place an order for 50 lbs of culled tomatoes. Those are late tomatoes that are not quiet perfect enough for retailing, they may have a spot or two on them, an odd shape, or not quite ripe, whatever! They are still fresh, local, organic tomatoes with tons of flavour and this is what I want, also the price is usually about half of the regular price. So I'll give you the tomato soup recipe for a smaller batch than the 50 lbs I usually buy, although I am sure after the first taste you'll wish you had made more, but there is always next year.

Most people like tomato soup, unfortunately most people don't make their own. I am going to share this recipe with you that will change your mind about ever again buying ready-made canned tomato soup. No offence to Mrs. Campbell, but canned soup is still canned soup no matter what you call it, and while you're at it, read the ingredient list! The beauty of this soup is that it starts as a great tomato sauce, so now you are killing two birds with one stone as the saying goes. We will start with the base or if you prefer the sauce which you can use fresh, preserve or freeze for use on pasta, pizza, vegetables etc. The base or sauce will be converted to become our tomato basil soup, the cost of both these dishes is very reasonable.

Tomato Sauce

20 cups

Ingredients:

15 lbs tomatoes, cut into quarters or smaller
5 medium onions, coarse chopped (slightly bigger than diced)
1 whole celery, coarsely chopped
6 peppers, coarse chopped
1 anise bulb coarse, chopped (also called fennel)
4 tablespoons crushed garlic (approx. 3 bulbs)
1 tablespoon thyme
4 tablespoons oregano
4 tablespoons dried basil
1 bunch parsley, chopped
2 teaspoons chili flakes
1 cup olive oil
4 cups water
Salt & pepper to taste

Method:

1. In a large 10-12 quart stockpot on medium heat, add the olive oil allowing it to get hot, barely smoking, then add the onions, celery, peppers, anise, stir well to sweat the vegetables for about 5 minutes or so.

2.   Now add your tomatoes, garlic and the rest of the herbs and the water. If your pot is too small and you can't get all of the tomatoes in all at once, just wait a few minutes until the tomatoes liquefy this will allow you to put the rest in. You now want your sauce to simmer covered for about 2 hours, stirring once in a while.

3.   By this time the aroma permeating your kitchen should have you convinced that it was all worth while. The next step is to use your hand blender and process the sauce to the consistency that YOU want, coarse, fine, whatever works best for you.

Now you have a wonderful organic tomato sauce for your pasta dishes for the future. I usually preserve my sauce in Mason jars; they keep extremely well but store them in a cool storage, as you should do with all preserves.

Tomato Basil Soup

4 servings

Now with our base tomato sauce let's convert it to a wonderful Tomato Basil Soup.

Ingredients:

4 cups homemade tomato sauce

2 cups chicken stock

1 cup fresh basil

Cream for garnish

Method:

1.   Bring 4 cups of the tomato sauce to a boil, reduce to a simmer, and then add 2 cups of chicken stock, and 1-cup of chopped fresh basil.

2.   Using your hand blender process until smooth as cream. Bring back to the boil and serve.

3. I usually like to dribble a teaspoon of whipping cream on top, it adds to the presentation and also kills some of the acidity of the soup.

4. If there are no children involved this soup can be converted to a tomato gin soup, by simply adding a tablespoon of gin on the bottom of each bowl, pouring the soup over it, and the cream on top of course. Now that's a soup that will make you a culinary whiz with your family and friends.

In 1963, I remember buying a food blender that cost me 3 weeks wages at the time. This was a state of the art blender 12 cups and all stainless; you could process a whole eggshell and it would all be pulverized beyond recognition, totally amazing. The beauty of such pulverization was that you could take any vegetable, meat, fish or whatever and blend it to a texture equal to that of baby food texture but this was homemade with all the nutrition and vitamins left intact as nature intended it to be. Needless to say my children never were given bought baby food to eat and we saved a lot of money. It's funny but that very same blender is making a comeback. One of the major super stores had a promotional display and I looked at the unit and by golly it had not been modified since the original 50 years ago. Which goes to prove *"if it isn't broken, don't fix it!"* Making a quick healthy soup with that blender is so easy. All you do is take any vegetables you want, cut into bite-size pieces, the more the better, add 2 quarts of stock, chicken or beef, the spices of your choice. Whiz it up for a couple of minutes, transfer to a saucepan, bring to the boil and serve. Now what could be simpler or healthier, not to mention the cost and time saving factor, so no more excuses for not making homemade soups.

There are certain tools in a kitchen that everyone should have, not a whole bunch of useless gadgets that don't work. One such gadget that comes to mind real quickly shows on TV how easy it is to chop onions, egg, garlic etc. Yes, but what they don't tell or show you is that it can only chop half an onion at a time, or three cloves of garlic, now that's practical isn't it? "But wait, if you call within the next ten minutes we will ship you absolutely free a second unit, you pay only the shipping and handling (I think it's about $20.00 so not so free). But millions are sold, only to rest in the back of your kitchen cabinet to end up someday in a garage sale. So forget useless gadgets, buy quality and only buy it once.

- A professional knife set will last you a lifetime.
- A high-end food processor is the best tool in your kitchen (commercial type).
- A hand blender for the smaller jobs that need processing.
- Kitchen pots and pans should last your lifetime, if you buy the right ones. Stainless, copper layered bottom give you the best heat transfer, which is what you want. If you must have non-stick, only use them for low heat frying, like frying eggs or making an omelet, because the Teflon coating has been shown to cause health problems when the coating separates from the pan and ends up in your food. The alternative, which is now available, is a ceramic coated pan which is very good because it will tolerate a much higher temperature than Teflon and it will last much longer.

Fall is my favorite time of the year, the temperature is mellow the air has a certain feel to it, almost peaceful and serene. This is the time also to go in the forest and become a hunter-gatherer looking for those elusive fungi. Mushroom picking is a great way to introduce your kids to the thrill of finding the food you're going to eat whilst enjoying quality time and teaching them to appreciate food that they have found and gathered and its also good exercise!

Chanterelle mushrooms are plentiful in our area of Vancouver Island, we also pick lobster, hedgehog, oyster and cauliflower mushrooms. Each time I find a cauliflower mushroom, no sooner have I picked it than I am already cooking it in my taste brain into a creamy pasta dish with fresh basil and a little cheese on top, what a treat. It's amazing the amount of territory you cover to gather a decent harvest, climbing steep hills amongst dead fallen trees and scrubs that seem to attack you. The reward of finding those morsels and the wonderful dishes you can create with them is well worth the effort and sore muscles the next day.

First crop of the season, fresh chanterelles

Chanterelle Mushroom Soup

6 servings

One of my favorites is chanterelle soup using my homemade chicken stock, this recipe will work with basically any variety of mushroom.

Ingredients:

5 lbs fresh chanterelles

2 medium onions, chopped

2 chopped shallots (optional)

4 tablespoons olive oil

1 cup chopped celery

1 teaspoon herbes de Provence

8 cups chicken stock

½ cup butter or margarine, melted

3 tablespoons flour

1 cup whipping cream or half & half

Salt & pepper

Pinch of nutmeg

Fresh thyme

Chopped parsley

**Optional 1 tablespoon Canadian Rye whiskey per bowl

Method:

1. Start with at least 5 lbs of fresh chanterelles, coarsely chopped.

2. Sweat chopped onions in the olive oil add shallots for that extra flavour if desired.

3. Add chopped celery and cook for about 5 minutes stirring all the time. Add herbes de Provence.

4. Add 8 cups of chicken stock and simmer for about 1 hour.

5. Cool and process until smooth.

6. Now at this stage you can either continue with the soup or put some aside for another day, because what you have so far is a concentrate of chanterelle soup base. So let's put half of the base in a plastic storage/ freezer bag and freeze it.

7. Bring the rest of the soup base to a light boil.

8. Add flour to melted butter or margarine and mix well. Then add this uncooked roux to the soup base and stir well. I like to use my hand blender for this.

9. After everything is well blended, add whipping cream, I know there is fat in there but this soup requires you to indulge (you can use half & half cream).

10. At this point season the soup to taste as far as salt and pepper is concerned and add nutmeg, thyme, and a little chopped parsley on top and voila.

11. **If children are not involved, in my soup bowl I'll pour 1 table-spoon of Canadian rye whiskey and pour the soup over it. Now you have a soup to die for! The rye whiskey gives the chanterelle soup an incredible new dimension.

In a good year we'll have enough chanterelle soup base to see us through the winter. And each time you make it, the earthy fragrance of fall comes back to your mind and reminds you of all the fun you had searching for the little morsels. If you have never tried picking chanterelles before I suggest you get a couple of friends and venture into the woods in the fall. Chanterelles are very easy to identify and there are various pocket books available that make it easy to recognize the various types of fungi in your area detailing the seasons, terrain, along with color pictures. Try it!

When cooking mushrooms, especially wild ones do not salt them while cooking; there is a lot of moisture in mushrooms and the salt draws out the flavours as well, so reduce the heat to cook slowly and evaporate the excess moisture. This way you'll retain the flavour of the mushrooms. Another thought, I am sure you have heard it many times "do not wash mushrooms they'll absorb water", not true if you wash them quickly but if you soak them that's a different story. I personally don't like the taste of manure in my food, because let's face it that is what commercial mushrooms are grown in, so I wash my mushrooms; a quick wash and toss in a colander will clean your mushrooms. With the wild ones, especially the chanterelles that seem to attract those pesky pine needles, I rinse them one at the time and lay them on a cookie sheet with a tea towel underneath, so that water can drip off. It's time consuming but well worth the effort and your chanterelles will keep better. I have kept them on the counter like that for over a week and they are fine.

I also dehydrate some of my chanterelles, they'll keep for a couple of years that way without losing flavour. I also put some of the dehydrated chanterelles in the food processor and reduce them to a fine powder, like table salt, and store it in a jar. When I am making an omelet I'll sprinkle a teaspoon or so of powdered chanterelle on top, this adds a great fragrance to my omelet. I also do the same when I am making a stew along with a few of the dehydrated ones. Another of my favorites is a chanterelle omelet with ditch weed, well at least that's what my friends call it what they really means is watercress. Yes, the wild stuff grows in ditches but only where the water flows constantly, which means clean water. The peppery taste of wild watercress and chanterelle in an omelet is a dish guaranteed to awaken your taste buds.

A New Life of Plenty

A few years after the war, when I was ten years old, my parents realized that there was no future in France for us and decided to immigrate to Australia to start a new life. The first few years were hard, not speaking the language and going to school, kids making fun of your clothes and accent and most of all trying to keep up to classroom level, when you don't understand everything that is being taught. I managed to get by and soon my family had a group of friends that had a lot in common with us, mainly that they loved good food, good wines and the outdoors. A Sunday morning ritual was born, we all met early at my family's home, decided where we were going and took off. Each family had decided during the week who was going to bring what. So one time you'd be responsible for the meat, next time it would be the vegetables and so on and of course we would all bring the most important thing, WINE.

One of my favorite picnics, as we would call them, was when we would buy a whole lamb and slow cook it on an open fire for about 3 hours. A half-hour before it was fully cooked we would gather green eucalyptus branches and put them in the fire. Great bellows of smoke would erupt, but most of all the fragrance of the lamb, the fire and the eucalyptus was enough to make you salivate.

The picnics in our newly adopted land were always full of great food and camaraderie. Most of the time we would pick a spot near the ocean, but other times we would venture inland where snakes, ticks, and deadly spiders resided. Our inland destinations always ended up close to a river or creek because there we could harvest a wonderful treat called "yabbies". I

Rack of lamb Provençal

am not sure about the spelling, but it's an Australian Aboriginal name for fresh water crayfish, mini lobsters in other words. To fish for them you first had to get a piece of meat, sheep lungs from a butcher were free and just right for the purpose. Then you let the piece of lung get let's say "mature"; putting a piece in a jar in the sun for a few days would do the trick. Next we made a triangular gadget with wire and wood on which you attached this "mature" piece of meat. The wire and wood contraption with bait in place was lowered to the bottom of the creek and left there for a couple of hours. After a couple of hours, we would very slowly raise it to the surface and there we would have a dozen or more of the mini lobsters just waiting to be picked. The pot of water was already boiling so within 5 minutes we were enjoying the fruits of our labor. Talk about fresh, and so tasty.

We have these freshwater crayfish here on Vancouver Island, but I have yet to get any that are big enough for my taste. Three inches is the biggest that I have caught so far, once the head is removed there is not much meat left, so for a feed you have to harvest a lot of them.

Australia introduced me to lamb. In France after the war, meat was scarce and very expensive, on the other hand in Australia, lamb was the cheapest of all meats at the time. That may explain why lamb to this day is my favorite meat. I would recommend buying local lamb, if you can, but New Zealand would be my second choice, before Australian which I find in general to be larger, fattier racks which leads me to believe that it's an older lamb. This seems to be the rule for Australian lambs, that they are older at killing time than the New Zealand ones; it only takes a few weeks more to make that difference. You may also notice the smell of lanolin to be stronger in the Australian lamb, which I find offensive.

Michel Rabu

Lamb Provençal

Serves 4

Ingredients:

2 lamb racks, frenched

2 tablespoons Dijon mustard

1 teaspoon sea salt or kosher

1 teaspoon herbes de Provence

1 cup breadcrumbs or panko (Japanese white bread crumbs)

1 full head of garlic

1 cup parsley

Method:

1. Preheat oven 425°F.

2. In a food processor, add the garlic, parsley and breadcrumbs, process to a fine mixture.

3. Using a pastry brush coat the racks of lamb on all sides with the Dijon then sprinkle with salt and herbes de Provence.

4. Spread the breadcrumbs onto a sheet of plastic wrap and roll the rack until fully coated. Press hard, so everything except the Frenched ribs are coated.

5. Wrap a piece of foil around the exposed ribs to prevent them from browning or burning.

6. Cook at 425°F for 15 minutes then let the rack rest out of the oven covered with foil wrap for at least 10 minutes before carving.

Garlic smashed potatoes, sautéed green beans, and ginger carrots would be a nice compliment to the lamb rack.

Seasoned Breadcrumbs

Whilst we are on the subject of making your own, let me share my recipe for making seasoned breadcrumbs.

I start by saving stale bread on a cookie sheet in a dry area, when I have enough to make a decent batch in my food processor I do the following. Put bread in chunks in the processor and pulse for a couple of minutes, add a bunch of fresh parsley, 3-4 cloves of garlic, and whatever spice I feel like usually herbes de Provence. Process for a couple of minutes. I put this all in a plastic storage/ freezer bag and freeze it, this way I always have ready to use seasoned homemade healthy breadcrumbs without MSG and other additives and again look at the money you have saved.

Now you can change a simple pork chop into a seasoned moist delicate dish. Just dip your pork chop into an egg wash, coat with your seasoned crumbs (right out of the freezer) and bake for 10 minutes @ 375°F. Done! The same can be done with chicken breast or fish. The breading helps to retain the moisture whilst cooking as well as releasing the garlic, and parsley flavour to your dish and adding another element of texture.

Aside from the money you save by making your own, it's the satisfaction of knowing that you control the product, as to what goes in to it, no added chemicals, preservatives etc. Keeping it healthy.

I look forward to each growing season when I can go to the farmers market and buy fresh, organic vegetables or fruits. To freeze, make jams, can peaches or pickle beets… The flavour derived from these is much better than store bought, and the reason is simple it's Fresh! Each time you open one of these cans or jars it reminds you of that time when you were making it and your smell and taste senses are reawakened. I know you may be thinking "Yes, that's fine and dandy, but who's got the time to do all of what you are suggesting?" We all do. Maybe all we need is to cut out a TV show twice a week, or take a couple of hours a week on your day off to prepare some of these suggestions. This actually will save you time down the road, and after all the benefits are definitely worth the effort. Healthier eating, money saving, helping the local farmers, lowering carbon footprint, better tasting food, lowering chemical ingestion, all positive moves to a better and healthier life.

Braised Lamb Shanks

Serves 4

Another cut of lamb that I enjoy is lamb shanks braised. This is a very reasonable dish to prepare and ideal as a fall or winter comfort dish. Full of flavour with root vegetables, and you can make it so that it's a one-dish dinner.

When cooking this dish don't be surprised if your neighbors all of a sudden are on your doorstep, wondering what you are cooking that smells so good.

Ingredients:

4 lamb shanks

1 medium rutabaga, cut bite-size

4 carrots, cut in half

2 medium onions, quartered

4 parsnips, cut in half lengthwise

4 small turnips, cut in half

4 celery stalks, cut in half

1 anise bulb, cut into quarters

2-500ml cans of diced tomatoes

2 cups chicken stock

1 tablespoon herbes de Provence

½ cup chopped parsley

2 whole bay leaves

10 garlic cloves, cut in half

½ cup olive oil

2 teaspoons sea salt

1 teaspoon coarse pepper

Method:

1. Set oven @325°F.

2. In a frying pan over medium heat, add the olive oil, when hot add the shanks and brown on all sides.

3. Place all the cut vegetables in a deep 9x12 baking dish.

4. Add tomatoes and chicken stock to the vegetables and, stir to coat them evenly.

5. Place the shanks on top of the vegetables and sprinkle the herbes de Provence, salt, pepper, add the bay leaf, and garlic.

6. Cover with foil, seal well as we want to retain all the moisture we can.

7. Cook for 1-½ hours minimum turning the shanks once. When done, the meat should look like it's ready to fall off the bone. Sprinkle the parsley just before serving.

This dish can be served with pasta or plain boiled potatoes. Any sauce left over can be frozen to use the next time you cook shanks, or as a sauce for pasta or root vegetables. A rustic bread like filone, or ciabatta is great to dip in the sauce, and let's not forget a nice bottle of cabernet sauvignon to wash all these flavours down.

If cooking this dish in the early spring check your garden to see if the dandelions are out yet, if so pick the young leaves to make a salad Just combine the leaves and a simple olive oil and garlic vinaigrette. If you're lucky enough to have access to ditch weed aka watercress, this will also work well, the natural bitterness of both of these salads, is a perfect pairing for the lamb shanks. I would recommend you do like the French people and have your salad after the lamb shanks. You will be surprised at the cleansing effect the salad has. I would also follow with a cheese tray to compliment the meal.

Curried Lamb

4 serving

Only once do I recall having a curry dish served to me outside from ordering it in a restaurant, yet each time I have served a curry dish to my guests the response has being very positive. So my guess is that most people are intimidated by having to make something as foreign as a "curry". I am going to share with you a very simple curry dish that I am sure will please. With lots of flavours and just the right amount of heat, and as far as cost, very reasonable to make. This recipe also works equally well using pork shoulder chops.

Ingredients:

3 lbs fresh lamb shoulders chops

4 shallots, chopped

4 garlic cloves, coarsely chopped

3 tablespoons fresh ginger, grated

2 tablespoons flour

¼ cup canola oil

4 tablespoons Madras curry

1 teaspoon green curry

1 teaspoon cumin

1 teaspoon coriander

1 cup sliced celery (sliced on a bias)

2 cups sliced carrots

2 cups chicken stock

1 can coconut milk

1 onion, sliced

1 cup pineapple juice

1 cup sliced green apple

1 cup sliced mango

¼ cup shredded coconut

¼ cup cilantro

Method:

1. Cut the chops into large bite-size pieces. Put them in a plastic storage/ freezer bag and add the flour and toss until all the pieces are well coated.

2. In a large pot, bring the oil to a high temperature (light smoke). Add the shallots and cook for a couple of minutes.

3. Add the lamb, cook whilst stirring. You want a light browning on the meat.

4. Add the garlic and both curries and stir well.

5. Add the chicken stock, pineapple juice, and coconut milk. The meat should be covered plus a half inch with the liquids, if not add a little more pineapple juice. Cover and reduce the heat to low simmer and let cook for half an hour.

6. Add celery, carrots and onion, cover and cook a further half hour.

7. Add the apples and mango and cook uncovered for a further 10 minutes.

8. Check for spice level, this is when you balance the flavour by adding more heat, salt or sweetness, what ever tastes best for you.

9. Before serving top with the chopped cilantro and sprinkle the shredded coconut all over.

I like to serve this dish over basmati rice, cooked in half pineapple juice and half water.

Pork is another food that aside from pork chops is not fully utilized in the home, yet it can be the most economical meat you can buy. Pork is leaner these days because of the way the pigs are raised, and the feed they are given. I usually buy whole pork loins when they are on sale and I cut a roast, some center cut chops. I cut some center chops about 1 inch thick to cook as is, and some ½-inch thick, which I pound between two sheets of plastic film to make schnitzels. With the trim and fat I make "rillettes" which are a very French appetizer; it looks like pâté, which you can spread, with lots of flavour and a great texture. To my amazement I found that young people just love this spread, I think it's because the fat is rendered to the point that you really don't taste it, and the texture is the other appeal! So as you can see buying a whole loin, cutting it, and working with it, can make you several meals at a very reasonable price.

Pork doesn't have to be cooked to the well-done stage anymore, medium is just right, this way you retain the moisture and maximize the flavours. I don't think that there's anything more unpalatable then an overcooked piece of pork. Letting the meat rest after cooking is especially important with pork this allows the moisture to permeate through the meat making it moist and tender. I'll share with you a couple of my favorite quick and easy pork dishes. Let's start with a pork loin roast.

Pork Loin Roast Dijon

Serves 4

Ingredients:

1 piece pork loin

2 tablespoons grainy Dijon mustard

1 teaspoon coarse salt

1 tablespoon herbes de Provence

1 cup chopped parsley

1 cup breadcrumbs

6 garlic cloves, cut in half

1 onion, quartered

Method:

1. Set oven @ 425°F.

2. With a sharp paring knife poke 12 holes in the top fat side of the loin, insert the garlic clove halves into them.

3. Mix breadcrumbs, ½ cup of the parsley and herbes de Provence together.

4. Spread the grainy Dijon mustard all over the loin, including the ends, and sprinkle the salt over it.

5. Spread a sheet of plastic film longer than the size of the roast. Distribute your breadcrumb mixture evenly over the plastic and roll the loin in the breadcrumb mixture making sure that the

Pork Loin

whole loin is well covered with the crumb mixture. Apply pressure while rolling.

6. Put a little oil in the bottom of a baking dish, place the roast in, add the quartered onion around the roast and bake until you get an internal temperature of 160°F or 71°C.

7. Let the roast rest for 10 minutes, covered with foil after removing from the oven before carving.

8. Serve with Dijonais sauce if desired — recipe follows.

As a compliment to this earthy dish, I like to vegetables cooked in another baking dish at the same time as the roast. Parsnips, carrots, rutabaga, onions, celery root, beets, squash, potatoes, any of these or all as I usually do. Just cut your vegetables into bite-size pieces, sprinkle them with olive oil and herbes de Provence and bake covered with foil. This stops the burning, and retains the moisture and flavour of each vegetable. Before serving sprinkle parsley all over the vegetables, try to keep your vegetables *al dente*. Enjoy!

Dijonais Sauce

If you want a sauce for your roast here is what you do.

Ingredients:

½ cup pork roast juices

1 cup sliced mushrooms

2 tablespoons Dijon mustard

½ cup dry white wine

½ cup whipping cream

1 tablespoon butter

1 tablespoon chopped parsley

Method:

1. In a frying pan, take ½ cup of the pan juices from your roast, add sliced mushrooms, and sauté for a couple of minutes.

2. Add the mustard, stir, then add the white wine, and cream. Stir well and reduce by half.

3. Remove from heat and add the butter and parsley and stir until glossy.

4. Pour the sauce over the sliced roast.

You can also use this sauce with leftover roast, simply make the above sauce, pour it over the sliced pork roast, and place in a 325°F oven for 5 minutes.

Indonesian Pork Tenderloin

Serves 2

Pork tenderloin comes on sale from time to time, usually in a pack of two or four fresh tenderloins. This certainly is the best cut of pork you can get, no fat, tender, quick to prepare and very tasty. Again do not overcook! This recipe has an Asian touch to it, you can marinate the meat the night before if you wish, this will only accentuate the flavour.

Ingredients:

1 pork tenderloin (allow 1 pork tenderloin for two person)

1 tablespoon fresh grated ginger

3 tablespoons kecap manis sauce

1 tablespoon chopped cilantro

Method:

1. Score the meat diagonally about 2 inches apart.

2. Mix the grated ginger and kecap manis sauce together.

3. With a pastry brush, brush the loin with the sauce, cover and keep refrigerated for at least 2 hours — overnight is best to maximize the flavours.

4. Bake at 425°F for 15 minutes. Let rest, covered, for 5 minutes before serving.

5. Cut portions on the diagonal and sprinkle with cilantro when serving.

It is quite safe now to serve pork medium to medium rare. As a side for the Asian flavoured pork loin I recommend a vegetable stir fry of ½ red onion cut length wise, carrots, celery, snap peas, bok choy, mushrooms, red peppers, along with jasmine rice or a steamed Asian noodle. This makes for a great meal that's fresh tasting and very healthy, colorful and easy to prepare. Any leftover cooked pork tenderloin, sliced thinly makes a great addition to a green salad the next day for lunch.

Schnitzel Dijonais

Serves 4

Instead of buying expensive pork loin chops, doing your own cutting will give you these chops plus much more for later meals.

Ingredients:

4 pork loin chops ½ inch thick

2 egg yolks

¼ cup whipping cream

breadcrumbs enough to coat

Canola oil

SAUCE:

2 tablespoons olive or canola oil

1 cup sliced mushrooms

2 shallots, chopped (onion will do if you don't have shallots)

½ cup white wine

½ cup chicken stock

½ cup whipping cream

1 teaspoon herbes de Provence

2 tablespoons Dijon mustard

1 tablespoon chopped parsley

Method:

1. Oven set at 325°F.

2. First we must bread the "schnitzels: Pound the ½ inch thick loin chops between plastic film to a thickness that doubles the size of the chop.

3. Mix a couple of egg yolks with the whipping cream.

4. Dredge the schnitzel into the cream mixture and then into the breadcrumbs.

5. In a frying pan, add enough canola oil to coat the bottom of the pan and bring the pan to a high temperature. Fry the pork for about one minute on each side, transfer to a dish in the oven at 325°F.

6. Now we make the sauce: In a separate frying pan add the oil, shallots, mushrooms and herbes de Provence, cook for about three minutes.

7. Add the white wine, chicken stock, and Dijon mustard, stir well and reduce by half.

8. Reduce the temperature to low/medium then add the whipping cream, stirring well until the sauce thickens this may take up to five minutes.

9. Pour the sauce over the schnitzels and top with the fresh parsley.

The same method can be used with chicken breast, just reduce the mustard by half so as not to overpower the chicken flavour.

As a side for the pork I like to do a one-pot pasta dish, rotini works well. Once the pasta is cooked al dente, add broccoli florets, or rapini, a small can of white beans and cook for about two minutes on medium heat. Add sun-dried tomatoes (optional), a small can of diced tomatoes and two or three cloves of chopped garlic. Drizzle some virgin olive oil on top, and sprinkle with shredded Parmesan and fresh chopped basil, stir well, put the lid on and let sit for 4-5 minutes before serving. Your vegetables will be crunchy, and you now have a side dish that has all the components for a healthy dinner. The fresh grated Parmesan along with fresh chopped basil adds a great finish to this great side. Again fast and easy, this dish reheats well in the microwave for next day's lunch.

Rillettes de Porc — Pork Spread

Whenever I am working to trim a pork loin I always have trimmings from the side seam and butt ends that have too much fat for me so what to do with this extra meat? Well there is a very French dish that calls for just that kind of meat "Rillettes de Porc" which translated means pulled pork spread. I have introduced this dish to several of my friends and grandchildren and all have asked for more. So I guess I should share this recipe with you, it's a form of pâté which is found everywhere in France and each region adds their particular nuances of the local flavour preferences.

Ingredients:

2 lbs pork trim (or pork shoulder)

8 shallots or three medium onions

½ bottle dry white wine (375ml)

1 whole garlic head, chopped

2 bay leaves

1 tablespoon black coarse pepper

2 tablespoons sea salt

1 cup chopped parsley

2 tablespoons herbes de Provence

3 tablespoons olive oil

Method:

1. Cut pork into 1" chunks.

2. In a large soup pot over medium heat, add olive oil and chopped shallots and stir for a couple minutes, do not allow to brown.

3. Add the pork and cook while stirring for 5-8 minutes.

4. Add the chopped garlic, white wine, bay leaves, herbes de Provence and salt and pepper. Cover the mixture with warm water -2" above the meat. Cover and simmer at a low boil for 1 hour.

5. Remove the cover after one hour and cook further until there is no liquid left. Be careful to stir every couple of minutes at this stage, you don't want the mixture to burn or stick to the bottom of the pot.

6. Once the mixture is free of any liquid add the chopped parsley.

7. Remove the bay leaves and with two forks shred the pork mixture until the meat is in a fine shredded state. This will take a good 10 minutes to accomplish this task, but that's the secret to a first class Rillette de Porc.

8. Check for seasoning at this stage, you may want to add more salt. I personally prefer a low salt content.

9. Press the mixture into an earthenware dish or several ramekins and cover with plastic film.

10. Chill overnight.

This will keep in the fridge for up to one month, but my experience tells me you'll be lucky if it sees the end of the week. The best and simplest way to enjoy Rillettes is spread on a piece of buttered French baguette along with Dijon mustard and of course let's not forget a glass of chilled dry white wine to go along, enjoy!

Being in the restaurant business for so many years you learn a thing or two about cooking. The most important is the "mise en place'" which translated from the French literally means "put into place" or simply "your set-up". In other words before you start cooking a given recipe you first must have everything laid out and chopped or sliced, whatever is required for this dish ready to use as you cook. You don't want to start cutting onions in the middle of a recipe or anything else for that matter. So having all ingredients in front of you, peeled, cut, sliced, ready to use, is "the mise en place". When you work in a restaurant you quickly learn that not having a "mise en place " done properly will cost you dearly during service! Cooking is the simplest of tasks if you are well set-up, that's why a good restaurant can serve 50 guests or more at the same time. Having fresh ingredients is the second most important asset, because you can be a great Chef, but without fresh and quality ingredients; your dish will not stand-up to culinary scrutiny.

Cooking should be fun, not a chore. Getting your partner or kids involved in preparing a meal can be a great learning experience for all. Plus they will have a greater appreciation of food because they took part in the process, as well as making them independent for meal preparation. For a man, being able to cook seems to have a certain appeal with women, maybe it takes the stress of "having to cook" away, knowing that eating in not solely dependent on one person being able to cook the meal. So if you can take that approach, I am sure cooking will become an art form of sort and be fun. "Having to cook or wanting to cook", will have different results in the food you prepare. It's almost like hate and love.

A word of caution I usually like to have my glass of wine close to me while cooking and one time I got carried away consuming more wine whilst cooking and then while eating. When dessert came around I was to make "crêpes suzette", a dish that I have done dozens of times. But not having done my "mise en place" for the crepes, I had to cut oranges and a lemon for the sauce. This is not recommended if you are inebriated; you do not want to handle knives at this time but I did, and somehow the knife slipped from the counter and landed though my foot. I was wearing floppies, again not recommended, even if you're sober, in the kitchen; footwear safety is a must. Needless to say I learnt my lesson that day.

Cooking has become more flexible in the last few years. The rules are less stringent; fusion cuisine is more commonly accepted, which I believe is great. You get to eat healthier, sauces are lighter, portions usually smaller, and a greater variety of crisp colourful vegetables to compliment dishes along with new intricate nuances of spices not related to the classics, not to mention the simplicity of cooking most dishes. I love a stir-fry made with chicken thighs, a variety of 8 or 9 vegetables, with fresh ginger, garlic, and sweet soya, and five spice (See the Spices and Rub Mixes section for the recipe). So simple and quick to prepare, and only one pot to wash, the wok, not to mention the fact that the chicken can be substituted with any other protein.

I have always enjoyed game: ducks, geese, venison, whatever I would go and hunt. When I moved to the farm and started raising fallow deer, I had to develop new recipes for the product, so that when I sold it at the farmers market I was able to give my customers easy recipes for them to try. This was a way to get repeat and satisfied customers. This was an advantage of being a Chef that other farmers didn't have, so my little farmers market stand became quite popular. People were always asking for all kinds of recipes. I love that kind of interaction with people.

Venison Medallions

Serves 4

This venison recipe is very simple to make and tastes just great.

Ingredients:

- 2 venison tenderloins, sliced on a bias 1-inch thick
- 4 shallots, chopped fine
- 1 lb mushrooms, sliced (mixed: oyster, chanterelles, portabello if available)
- ¼ lb butter (no substitute, you must indulge this time)
- ½ cup Madeira wine (Marsala)
- ½ cup whipping cream
- 1 teaspoon herbes de Provence
- ½ cup beef stock
- 2 tablespoons chopped parsley

Method:

1. Set oven @ 300°F.

2. In a large frying pan melt the butter, holding back 1 tablespoon, add the shallots and cook for a couple of minutes on medium heat. Do not allow to brown.

3. Add the herbes de Provence and mushrooms and cook a further 5 minutes.

4. Push all aside, turn the heat to high and add the meat. Cook for two minute on each side.

5. Pour the Madeira over the meat and then remove it from the pan and set aside in a warm oven.

6. Bring the heat back down to medium, add the beef stock and whipping cream and reduce until the sauce has thickened.

7. Add the tablespoon of butter and stir well this will make the sauce glossy and silky.

8. Add the meat and spoon the sauce over it.

9. Plate and sprinkle the chopped parsley over.

Asparagus wrapped in prosciutto ham and baked in garlic butter for just 5 minutes is a great vegetable side that goes well with this dish. So are rosemary-roasted potatoes, along with dill carrots and let's not forget the wine, preferably one with a strong character, Bordeaux, shiraz, or a good Cabernet.

Canard a L'Orange

Serves 2

Duck has always been intimidating to most but when you can buy de-boned duck breast, cooking duck has become a breeze. This recipe is a modern version of the classic time consuming canard a l'orange and can be ready in just 15 minutes

Ingredients:

2 de-boned duck breasts (usually found in the frozen department)

3 finely chopped shallots

1 tablespoon olive oil

1 tablespoon brown sugar

1 tablespoon balsamic vinegar

1 tablespoon frozen orange juice concentrate

Juice and zest of one orange

1 tablespoon butter

1 tablespoon chopped parsley

Method:

1. Set oven to 375°F.

2. Score the fat side of the duck breast 3-4 scores diagonally making sure to score the fat only.

3. In a frying pan on medium heat, warm olive oil. Add the duck breast, fat side down and cook 2-3 minutes until fat side is brown.

4. Add the shallots and cook for a couple minutes.

5. Remove the breasts from the pan and put them in the oven for 8-10 minutes or until medium rare.

6. Add sugar, orange juice concentrate, and fresh orange juice to frying pan and stir to combine. Cook for a couple minutes until the sauce starts to thicken.

7. Add the balsamic vinegar and stir.

8. Add the butter and orange zest, stir and reduce.

9. At this stage add salt and pepper to taste. You may want more acidity or more sweetness, so add a little balsamic vinegar or brown sugar as needed.

10. Remove duck breast from the oven and slice on the bias about ¼ inch thick and pour sauce over the breasts and sprinkle with parsley.

A nice full-bodied red goes well with this dish.

Duck Breast with Berry Gastrique

Serves 4

Ingredients:

4 duck breasts

1 tsp herbes de Provence

Salt & pepper to taste

4 shallots

1 cup balsamic vinegar

1 cup sugar

4 cups berries, fresh is best but frozen also works (Any variety, I like a three berry mix)

1 pear, sliced

4 roasted beets

Arugula for four

Method:

1. Set oven to 375°F.

2. Score the duck breast on the fat side and season with the herbes de Provence and salt & pepper.

3. In a saucepan combine the sugar, and shallots and melt to a light caramel stage over medium heat.

4. Add the vinegar and berries. Slow simmer until reduced by half. Then strain and keep warm.

5. Roast the beets with skin on, then cool, peel and cut into four pieces.

6. Add the beets to the gastrique.

7. Slice the pear into ¼ inch slices, lengthwise, pan fry until carmelaized on both sides. Set aside.

8. Fatside down sear the duck breasts until golden, then remove and place in a dish in the oven for ten minutes or until medium rare. Remove from oven and let rest for a couple of minutes then slice on the bias.

9. Arrange arugula on the plates, add beets,pear slices and duck slices.

10. Drizzle all over with gastrique.

A glass of Pinot noir would go well with this dish. For sides, blanched baby bok choy and ginger carrots is all you need

GASTRIQUE SAUCE

A gastrique is a reduction of vinegar or other acid (cider, citrus juice, wine) with sugar, and usually a fruit. It begins by caramelizing the sugar over heat, then adding the fruit, then reducing the sauce while adding the vinegar.

Some sauces are then served as is, others are strained to remove the fruit pulp, making the sauce clear. A plain gastrique can also serve as a base for other sauces, such as a tomato sauce. The sauce is typically served with meat or seafood to add a fruit complement to round out the dish.

During my visit to France in the mid 90's, my family in Brittany wanted to get everyone together for a special family reunion dinner. Well easier said than done, for they are scattered all around the province and each one wanted to host the event in their area. They asked me what I would really like to eat, thinking he'll say seafood for sure. But since this was at the beginning of my one month stay, I figured I would be eating seafood the rest of the time, and also was keeping in mind that a seafood dinner for 27 of us would be very costly, so I said "you know I haven't had good potée since I can even remember so how about that." Well I got some very strange looks at first but then I noticed some of them starting to salivate at the thought of a potée. After all it's not the kind of dish that you would cook unless you had a dozen or more guests to impress, so like me most of them hadn't had a good potée for years.

One of my cousins found a farmhouse restaurant, located in an area that suited everyone, that specialized in "Potée Traditionelle" which came highly recommended. We phoned only to find out that the only day that worked for all of the family, was the day that the restaurant was closed, "good old Murphy" seems to follow me around. However, when the restaurant owner heard the magic number of 28 guests all of a sudden he wanted to know more about our intentions for that evening. We of course told him that we all enjoyed our wine, Champagne, Cognac, and that this dinner was for a special guest that came from Canada especially to try his potée. Well that changed everything. He would be only too happy to open for us and guaranteed us the use of the whole restaurant for us to enjoy.

A potée is a very old country, farm dish. To make a good potée you need to put a lot of love into the preparation. It's time consuming, the freshness of the vegetables is crucial, as well as the proper selection of the various meats that go into it. You must also have a big pot, now I mean BIG! When I give you the ingredient list you'll see what I mean but it's well worth it if done properly. I recommend a potée as a "must do" next time you're in France.

This restaurant did it in the traditional way, a huge cast iron pot which could hold about 40 litres or more of liquid and was suspended on a metal swing bracket in a huge farmhouse wood burning fireplace, this contraption is called a "Crémaillere". My grandmother had such a system and I remember seeing her crémaillere, always on the fire and usually soup or a stew would be simmering for hours on end, filling the whole farmhouse with an aroma of fresh vegetables and chicken or pork. So very simple, yet so amazingly wonderful, flavours would develop that can only be achieved with fresh products and slow simmering for hours.

I am going to give you a modified version of a potée keeping in mind that most of us don't have the huge pot needed to cook one, so I am keeping the number of portions small. Still, by the time you're finished you'll be able to serve at least 8-10 guests, and any leftover can be converted to a nice healthy soup. So look for the biggest soup pot you have.

Potée Traditionelle de Bretagne

Serves 8-10

This dish is very easy to make, all it takes is time, the freshest ingredients and the biggest stockpot you have.

Ingredients:

4 onions, quartered

6 medium carrots, cut into 2 inch logs

1 celery root (celeriac), cut into bite-size pieces

4 small turnips, cut into bite-size pieces

1 medium rutabaga, cut into bite-size pieces

8 yellow flesh potatoes, quartered

6 leeks, cut into 4-inch pieces

4 medium parsnips, cut into bite-size pieces

1 green cabbage, quartered

6 shallots

2 whole garlic heads, peeled

4 lb chuck beef roast

1 lb salted side pork, cut into bite-size pieces

2 lb Italian sausages (hot)

4 chicken drumsticks

8 chicken thighs

1 smoked ham hock

4 bay leaves

2 tablespoons herbes de Provence

1 tablespoon sea salt

2 tablespoons black pepper

1 cup chopped parsley

1 teaspoon dried savory (optional)

1 teaspoon dried oregano

2 cup dry white wine

½ cup olive oil

Method:

1. Set the oven @ 300°F.

2. Heat olive oil in pot on high heat, and brown the chuck roast. This will take about 5 minutes, you want to get a good caramelized coating on all sides. Transfer to a dish and place in the oven.

3. In the same pot, add salted pork and sausages, cook and brown for 4-5 minutes, transfer to dish in the oven.

4. Now do the same with the chicken legs, and thighs.

5. Once all the meats have being browned, add the white wine to the pot to de-glaze, use a wooden spatula to scrape all the good little bits of brown stuff from the bottom of the pot.

6. Put all the browned meats except for the chicken pieces back into the pot and add the smoked pork ham hock.

7. Add enough water to cover the meat plus an extra inch, add bay leaf, herbes de Provence, garlic, shallots, oregano, pepper, salt, and savory, cover and simmer for 1 hour.

8. After one hour, add potatoes, parsnips, rutabaga, onions, carrots, turnips, and add more hot water to over all the ingredients. Cook for a further 45 minutes.

9. Add the cabbage, leeks and chicken pieces and simmer for another 30 minutes.

10. The best way to serve this dish is to use a spider strainer or large slotted spoon to put all of the ingredients on a big platter. Sprinkle with chopped parsley and drizzle with a little olive oil

Serve with some fresh baked rustic bread, along with Dijon mustard to eat with the meats and a hearty Burgundy red wine. Now that's a full meal! The stock that is left over will make a base for great winter soup stock, so make several containers and freeze.

Another dish from the stew family that I really enjoy is a Beef Bourguignon. Again a straightforward dish, only the name sounds complicated so I'll share with you my version for this recipe. The first mistake people make is to buy expensive cuts of meat, what you are looking for in meat for this dish is maximum flavour and flavour comes with a little fat. I know it's a dirty word, but if you cook it properly the fat will be reduced to nothing, only the flavour will stay behind. I suggest either blade or chuck roast, cut it into 2-inch cubes, saving the bones and extra fat for making beef stock. The secret to making this particular cut of meat tender is the marinade, which is simple. Combine red wine, a little crushed garlic and herbes de Provence; cover and refrigerate for a day. The acid and enzymes in the red wine will breakdown the fiber and you'll be amazed how that beef will become tender after cooking.

Beef Bourguignon

4-6 servings

Chuck or blade roast is used here because it gives you the most flavour and the meat doesn't fall apart while cooking, yet because of the braising cooking method the meat will be tender. If you have a cast iron, Dutch oven, this is what you want to use.

Ingredients:

4-5 lb chuck or blade roast, cut into 2-inch cubes

2 tablespoons crushed garlic

1 teaspoon herbes de Provence

2 onions, quartered

2 tablespoons flour

1 quart beef stock

3 cups dry red wine (750ml bottle)

1 small can tomato paste

½ lb bacon, chopped

½ cup olive oil

½ cup butter

4 medium carrots 1-inch thick slices

2 bay leaves

½ lb pearl onions, peeled (buy the pickled ones, faster)

Salt and pepper to taste

Method:

1. Put the cubed meat in a stainless or ceramic bowl, but not aluminum. Add the herbes de Provence, crushed garlic, the quartered onions, and wine, stir. Cover and marinate overnight or longer.

2. When ready to cook, strain the meat mixture and put marinade aside. Put just the meat in a plastic storage/ freezer bag, add the flour, seal and toss until the flour has coated the meat.

3. On medium heat, cook the bacon in a Dutch oven or large pot, with the olive oil and quartered onions.

4. When the bacon is cooked, add the butter and when melted, add the beef and brown for about 5 minutes.

5. Add the beef stock and reserved wine marinade along with the tomato paste, stir well and cover. Simmer at a slow boil for 45 minutes.

6. Add the carrots, bay leaves, and pearl onions and cook for a further 30 minutes. At this stage of the game you have the option of cooking potatoes with the stew if you wish since we need to cook a further 30 minutes. I also enjoy the flavour of parsnips in my stew so this is when I would add them.

7. Add salt and pepper to your taste and serve.

Again a slice of a rustic loaf of bread to dunk in the sauce, complimented with a glass or two of a Chilean Merlot, what can I say!

O' Canada

February 1958, we arrived in Winnipeg minus 32 degrees below zero…
welcome to our new home! Don't get me wrong we loved Winnipeg, it had
a vibrant cultural society and friendly people. During the fifteen years we
were there, we established five beauty salons and two hairdressing schools.
Also this is where my sister, Joelle, was born.

My kids were just babies when I purchased a 10 acre hobby farm just
outside the city limits. This was during the Cold War, the news kept
warning us of the possible nuclear holocaust and how to survive by building underground shelters, stashing enough food and water for a year etc.
Well I thought that a small farm would be my way of surviving should this
ever happen.

We started by buying day old chickens and raising them for meat. My
son's responsibility was to feed these birds twice daily with grain and the
rest of the time they would forage around the property. Come fall we set
up a slaughtering area where we built a contraption to hang the birds from
after we had chopped their heads off so that they would bleed out properly.
After the birds had bled out, we would dip them in a cauldron of hot water
for about a minute and then we would start to pluck them, this was the
easiest part of the process. The next steps were the eviscerating, cleaning,
bagging and freezing of the birds. Thirty birds a day was pretty well our
limit, so with 100 birds to process we were kept busy for a couple of days,
but you know it was worth it. We would sell about 40 of the birds to family
and close friends, this way we would recover the total cost of feeding the
birds to maturity. After the first year the demand for our chickens from
those that had tried them was overwhelming, but not wanting to become
commercial we stuck to our 100 birds per year with a first come first serve

policy. The flavour of those birds was amazing; the skin cooked crisp and golden, the carcass bones made the most wonderful stock.

We also raised a few ducks, a couple of turkeys, a couple of lambs and a pig. I must tell you about our pig experience. I had a friend who was Moroccan and when he heard I was going to kill the pig he asked me what I was going to do with the blood, well I said I never thought about it so he suggested we make blood sausage. He said he would help me since he had done it several times before in is homeland, so I said sure let's do it! Since I was working till 1 pm the day of the scheduled pig killing, he offered to help with the peeling and cooking of the 20 lbs of onions required for the blood sausage. I arrived at home around 2pm that day, ready to kill the pig and make the blood sausage and to my surprise there's cooked onions all over my driveway.

"What the @##... happened", I said to my friend. Well he said "After the onions were cooked I put them in a pillowcase and tied the end of them. I put the pillowcase full of cooked onions on the driveway and put a piece of plywood on top and drove my car over them so as to mash them up for the sausage". Unfortunately, the pillowcase gave way, and so we had onions all over the driveway. We laughed and then cried as we peeled another 20lbs of onions. By the time we got the blood sausage made and cooked it was 5am. Mind you we didn't care too much since all that hard work required some heavy libation to keep us going. I tell you it's fun but cleaning the guts to make casing for the sausage is time consuming, but the result and taste of fresh blood sausage at 5 am with a glass of red wine was nothing less than brilliant. Definitely one for the "Brain Taste" memory file.

When I retired, in the late nineties, I went to work for a friend that has a beautiful 170 acre ocean front farm with a garden and greenhouse. He asked me to come and manage the farm and put something together that will make money. Wow! I was back in my element growing fresh quality food. The main commercial element of the farm was raising fallow deer, which was new to me but very challenging and interesting. I found a market for that meat and eventually we sold about 250 deer a year. I made "pâte" sausages, pepperoni, and special cuts for the restaurant industry. The products became very popular, when people realized how tasty and lean the deer meat was. For the first few months I had to give recipes on how to cook the meat to make sure they derived the best flavour and texture from the products. For most people this was all very new for them to cook farmed venison. I must say it was very gratifying to see people come back week after week and buy more products from us at the farmers markets that we attended each week in two different cities on Vancouver Island, Campbell River and Courtenay.

After a few months my "Brain Taste" said "remember the taste of those chickens you used to raise many years ago!" so I decided to raise a few as well. I started with 100 and raised them the same way I had done some 40 years before. The taste was the same, so I started to sell them at the local farmers market, next thing I knew I had more orders than I knew what to do with. The additional sales coming from those who had bought before. Now I was producing batches of 250 and selling out before they are ready for market, a nightmare! All that plucking, eviscerating, blood and guts everywhere and then when you're finished the sanitation process requirements would be very testing and time consuming as well. So batches of 250 birds became the maximum that my staff or I were prepared to handle, although the market demand could have handled three or four times that production. We had several customers that would order 30-50 chickens in the fall from us to fill their freezers for the winter. If ever you get a chance to raise your own chickens don't hesitate, it's well worth the effort.

Tarragon Chicken

4 servings

I like to use boneless breast with the wing drumette attached, this is strictly for presentation, this dish is quick, easy, tasty, great for when you have company that you want to impress. You can use breasts only, or cut up thighs and legs, whatever works for you.

Ingredients:

3 tablespoons olive oil

4 boneless chicken breast (option with drumette attached) or *thighs or legs

1 tablespoon cornstarch

1 teaspoon herbes de Provence

1 shallot, chopped

1 lbs mushrooms, sliced (shiitake, porcini, chanterelle, oyster, any or all)

½ cup fresh tarragon chopped or pickled

1 cup Chardonnay wine

½ cup chicken stock

1 cup whipping cream (you can substitute with yogurt)

Salt and pepper

Chopped parsley to sprinkle on top before serving

Method:

1. Set the oven at 350°F.

2. Put the four chicken breasts in a plastic storage/ freezer bag, add the cornstarch and herbes de Provence. Seal and shake vigorously. The reason for the cornstarch is simply to seal the meat to retain the juices, and to give a crisp coating to the meat, especially if you are using skinless breasts. I personally prefer to cook with the skin on this helps to retain the moisture in the chicken. And it also adds more flavour to the sauce, but it's all a matter of personal choice.

3. Add olive oil to a sauté pan and get it fairly hot. Put in the chicken breasts, skin side down first and sear for about 4 minutes on each side or until golden brown, remove breast from pan and put them in a dish in the oven at 350°F for about 10 minutes.

4. In the same frying pan, add mushrooms and shallots, cook for about 5 minutes, add more oil if necessary.

5. Add the wine to de-glaze the pan, get all those juice bits that are stuck on the bottom, use a spatula to scrap them off.

6. Now add your chopped tarragon and stir for a couple of minutes then add your chicken stock and reduce the temperature to low and continue to cook so as to reduce the sauce by half.

7. Add your cream or yogurt and stir well.

8. Take your cooked chicken breasts and put 3 diagonal scores on them, but don't cut through the breast all the way you want the it to stay whole, just scored so that the sauce will penetrate the flavour through out.

9. Add the juices, from the chicken whilst it was in the oven, to your sauté pan sauce, and stir. Salt and pepper to taste.

10. Place chickens breasts in a baking dish and pour the sauce all over them, return dish to the oven and bake for 10 minutes more.

11. Before serving, spoon sauce over each breast and sprinkle with parsley.

*If using chicken thighs or legs instead of breasts follow the same procedure but allow more cooking time, increase by at least 10 more minutes in the oven.

Steamed asparagus, gingered carrots, roasted yam as sides works well (careful not to over steam the asparagus, a few minutes at the most). You could also substitute the asparagus with fresh green beans sautéed in a little butter, garlic and de-glazed with lemon juice, topped with chopped parsley.

Oyster harvesting with my sons, Yanik and Daniel,
in Nootka Sound, British Columbia, Canada

Seafood

Being raised near the ocean, any kind of seafood is my favorite. Any kind, anytime, anywhere; I have been known to go out at night to gather some fresh oysters, we're talking late at night, like midnight or later. Some of the best winter tides are late at night and very low, which exposes some small tasty oysters that rarely get to be out of the water, consequently they have a very special taste and firmer texture; it's worth getting cold and wet for these little morsels. By the time I get home it could be as late as 4am, but still not too late to open a couple of dozen with a glass of dry white wine, and a piece of baguette bread then I sleep like a content baby. Good thing this type of excursion only happens a couple times a year.

During the summer we sometimes go to the West Coast of the island, specifically to Nootka Sound, and there I have found a spot for oysters that's rather unique. It's at the end of an inlet and there is a fresh water creek that feeds that bay, so you have fresh water on top of the salt water. As the tide goes down the oysters have to ingest this fresh water mix, which in return gives them a very special sweet taste, also the texture is more delicate, these oysters are to die for! We usually put out the prawn trap and harvest West Coast spotted prawns, these while still alive end up in a frying pan with butter, olive oil, garlic and fresh lemon juice and a good sprinkle of chopped parsley. Now that's the way to really taste the true flavour of these prawns, of course you mustn't forget the glass of white wine to go along with it! This is so simple yet so enjoyable. I am very fortunate to be able to fish and to have friends that always share their bounty with me. This ensures us of great fresh seafood all the time.

Panko Crusted Fish

Serves four

With the exception of Bouillabaisse, one of my specialties with seafood, I try to keep all other recipes as simple as I can, especially when the catch is fresh. This recipe works well with either, snapper, cod, halibut or even sole. We are going to use panko, a Japanese white breadcrumb that stays really crisp while cooking.

Ingredients:

2 cups panko (Japanese white bread crumbs)

4 pieces filleted white fish

¼ cup olive oil

2 eggs, beaten

1 cup flour

Zest and juice of one lemon or lime

Salt and pepper to taste.

1 tablespoon butter

2 tablespoons chopped parsley

Method:

1. Heat oven to 325°F.

2. Mix the salt, pepper and lemon zest with the flour.

3. Dredge the fish in the flour, then dip the fillet in the egg wash, and then into the panko crumbs, pressing lightly to make sure that the fish is well coated with the panko.

4. Fry the fish in the olive oil in a fairly hot frying pan for about two minutes on each side or until the fish is a light golden brown in colour.

5. Put the frying pan in the oven. Make sure the frying pan handle is not rubber or plastic that can't take the heat of the oven. Now the time in the oven is dependent on the thickness of the fish fillet, test by pressing your finger on the fish, it should feel almost spongy.

6. When you take the fish out of the oven remove it from the pan and place on a serving dish.

7. To the frying pan, add 1 the butter, the juice of the lemon and the chopped parsley, stir and when the butter starts to foam pour over the fish and serve.

For another version of this dish, you can add some crushed capers to the butter and lemon sauce for that extra flavour layer.

If you don't want the butter sauce, another alternative is topping the fish with a mango lime or peach salsa, this is a very nice refreshing light combination and low on fat and calories. If using salsa as a topping use fresh cilantro instead of the parsley.

Living on the coast of British Columbia, salmon is always available to us fresh, wild or farm raised. The wild caught is of course seasonal, but the farmed salmon is available year round and the quality has improved greatly, mainly because of the feed and antibiotic restrictions that have being imposed on fish farms. Also having pristine fast flowing waters like we have certainly helps in developing quality fish and producing a sustainable fishery at the same time, which also is reflected in the price we pay for this product. I still believe wild caught is best by far, but I am not opposed to farmed salmon and I do buy it when the wild stock is not available.

I am going to share with you some of my favorite ways of preparing salmon, in all cases you must be using fresh fish, remember if it smells fishy, it's not fresh. It should smell clean, sweet and the flesh should not be slimy or sticky, but be firm to the touch and with bright colour. The most important thing to remember when cooking fish, especially salmon: DO NOT OVERCOOK IT! If you do overcook your fish, it will be dry and bland; salmon needs moisture to retain its flavour and good texture.

I find that when children don't like fish it is because they have always had it overcooked and they don't find it palatable. Texture is very important to children's food; they can detect the slightest bit of fat for example, that adults wouldn't notice. I found this out when running the farm and I was feeding venison to children that were attending summer camps with us, and how all of them just loved it. The reason being, no fat, undercooked, good texture and flavour. Since then I have made it a point to observe this theory, and to date it has proved to be accurate.

Baked Whole Salmon

Serves 5-6

I like to do this on the BBQ, mainly because of the high temperature I can get from it 500°F, but I see no problems in using the oven.

Ingredients:

5-6 lbs salmon

2 lemons

1 onion

Olive oil

Salt and pepper

Method:

1. Heat BBQ.

2. Wash the fish, especially the cavity, make sure there is no blood anywhere, this would impart a bitter flavour when cooking.

3. Get a piece of aluminum foil large enough to wrap the fish, in other words, twice the total length of the fish and a bit more to seal the ends about 8 inches.

4. Slice the lemons and onion as thin as you can. Place the sliced onion in the cavity of the salmon along with a half dozen slices of lemon, salt and pepper.

5. Coat both sides of the fish with olive oil, place fish on its side, on the foil and place the remaining lemon slices on top of the fish, wrap the fish in the foil and seal both ends well. We don't want the steam to escape, as it will retain all the flavour that we want to concentrate while cooking.

6. Cook for 12-14 minutes on each side for this size fish. Remove from the fire. DO NOT OPEN the foil. Let it rest for 10 minutes.

7. After the 10 minutes of rest, open the foil and the skin should peel off easily from the top and bottom skin. Should it stay stuck to the foil, use a spatula along the backbone.

8. Once you have served the top part, you should be able to pull the rib bone off by hand.

9. Serve portions that will be moist and flaky.

Another very tasty variation to this recipe is to replace the lemon slices with thinly sliced anise (fennel root), this gives a light licorice flavour to the fish and also becomes an extra vegetable to serve.

Westcoast Prawns

Two Fish in Phyllo

Serves 4

This recipe is always a success at a dinner party, it looks elegant and tastes very different. I created this recipe many years ago for the Knowledge Network fundraising program, which asked Chefs to submit a new creation that they would select for their cookbook. My recipe was one of the ones selected and became a favorite at my restaurant. Again this is very simple to execute, but the key is fresh fish.

Ingredients:

1 box of phyllo pastry, thawed

4 pieces of fresh salmon, cut into 1-inch strips

4 pieces of halibut, cut into 1-inch strips

½ cup melted margarine

1 cup mango salsa (make your own or buy ready made)

1 bunch fresh cilantro, coarsely chopped

Method:

1. Make sure phyllo is thawed then preheat oven to 375°F.

2. Lay one sheet of phyllo on a sheet of plastic film. Brush on the margarine lightly. Add a couple of pieces of cilantro at random, add another sheet of phyllo on top, brush on more margarine and more cilantro, add your third and last sheet of phyllo on top.

3. Cut the phyllo sheets in half, length wise, this will give you two portions.

4. Place one piece of salmon at the end of the phyllo sheet, and put the halibut piece on top of the salmon.

5. Add a teaspoon or so of the salsa on top of the halibut.

6. Fold both sides of the phyllo sheets towards the fish and roll until you have used up all of the phyllo. It should look like a spring roll,

but a little thicker in diameter. Just before the last roll, brush on some margarine to seal the end, and then brush margarine all over the phyllo.

7. Repeat this process for the next three portions.

8. Place on a non-stick cookie sheet or foil coated with non-stick spray.

9. Bake for about 10 minutes or until golden brown.

10. Let rest for a couple of minutes and just before serving top with a little salsa, and cilantro.

The combination of the crisp phyllo, moist salmon, flaky halibut and fresh cool salsa with cilantro makes this a wonderful refreshing and new approach to serving fish. I am sure you'll enjoy this dish as much as I do.

You can change the type of fish you use. For example you may want to use a snapper and sole combination, or halibut and a shrimp puree, or salmon and scallops, even halibut and cold-smoked salmon (for this combination I would wrap the halibut with the smoked salmon since the salmon is thinly sliced this will accentuate the flavour throughout the halibut). As you can see it's all about taste and imagination, so put your "Brain Taste" to work!

Kecap Manis Salmon

Serves 4 per fillet

This Asian inspired and so simple salmon recipe creates a whole new layer of flavour. This dish lends itself to being served with plain steamed rice, and stir-fried vegetables. This means your preparation time is very quick and the end result very healthy. First you need to get some kecap manis, Indonesian sweet soy sauce, from your supermarket, if available. I find that the specialty Asian food stores usually have a better price than the larger super stores.

You can use salmon steak, or a whole fillet for this recipe. You simply brush kecap manis sauce on the fish and let stand in the refrigerator for at least 1 hour before frying or baking. I recommend that you fast fry the fish for a couple of minutes on each side and then finish it in the oven, the reason is that the kecap manis coating will have a tendency to burn on a

stovetop. After you have pan seared it, 10 minutes in the oven at 375°F should be just right to finish cooking the fish. Remember overcooked fish will be dry, best to be undercooked if anything. This also works well with halibut or snapper.

The suggested stir-fry for the above dish is quite simple and fast. Start with a little oil in a wok, get the temperature quite hot. Add your hard vegetables first, like onion, carrots, celery, cauliflower, then your mushrooms, snap peas, broccoli, and bok choy. Make sure that all vegetables are bite-size. The variety of vegetables you use in the stir-fry is strictly your choice, you can start with just three varieties, let you palate guide you. Once you have all the vegetables that you want to use in your stir-fry, toss a few times. At this point, you may want to add a flavour to some chicken stock, such as curry, soy sauce, ginger, garlic, kecap manis, sweet chili sauce, or all of the above to create a layer of truly Asian nuances to your stir fry. Add a tablespoon of cornstarch to the mixture and mix well, this will thicken your sauce a little. Add the chicken stock mixture to the vegetables and toss or stir a few times to make sure all the vegetables are well coated. Cover and cook for 4-5 minutes only; you want the vegetables to retain their colour and vitamins, so they should be crunchy when served. A handful of chopped cilantro and green onion sprinkled on top before serving will add colour and flavour to your dish.

West Coast Bouillabaisse

Serves 4

The true bouillabaisse can only be made in the Mediterranean area, it calls for specific fishes which are not available in North America, so I have come up with a version that can be made with local products and still be very close to the original.

Ingredients:

1 lb Manila clams

1 lb fresh mussels

1 lb fresh snapper

1 spotted prawns

1 Dungeness crab or substitute with 1 lb lobster

1 lb fresh or frozen scallops

½ cup olive oil

2 cups vegetable stock

1 fennel bulb, sliced ¼ inch thick

1 medium carrot, sliced 1 inch thick

4 medium onions, quartered

4 medium white potatoes, quartered (blanched for 5 min & drained)

4 garlic cloves, whole

1-750ml bottle of white wine

4 oz brandy

4 oz Pernod

1 good pinch of Spanish saffron (no substitute)

1-750ml can of diced tomatoes

Salt & pepper to taste

Method:

1. In a large pot (8 quarts) on medium, add the olive oil, garlic, onions, carrot, and fennel, and sweat for 5-10 minutes.

2. Cut the crab body into four pieces; score the legs, do the same if using lobster.

3. Add the brandy and Pernod to the crab mixture and stir well.

4. Add the saffron and wine and simmer for 5 minutes.

5. Add the potatoes, tomatoes, and the rest of the seafood.

6. Cook until the clams & mussels have opened, approximately 5 minutes.

7. Serve in a shallow bowl with lots of sauce and French bread and an aioli, made of homemade mayo with lots of crushed garlic and paprika.

A Culinary Odyssey

On a to France, in 2011, with my friend, Paul and his wife Maggie, and some friends from Majorca, Tom and Marinette, we hired a 43 feet long U-drive river boat for three weeks and went cruising down the Burgundy Canal. This is an experience that I highly recommend. This vessel had lots of room, queen size beds, a full galley, shower, bath, a sundeck topside, bicycles and a diesel motor that went all day at 8 mph and you couldn't even hear it!

The best part of the trip was the fact that you could stop anywhere, anytime. The canal has a road alongside for pedestrians or bicycle riders and the local, friendly baker came alongside each morning in his old beaten-up van beeping his horn at 7am. He was stocked full of wonderful goodies such as, fresh baked croissants, chocolate brioches, tarte au pommes and an incredible assortment of fresh baked bread from his wood fired ovens. Each day he would meet us no matter where we were, and of course we would reward him by buying a lot more than we should.

Along the canal if you travel 10 km you're into another town or village and usually each of these towns have a traditional specialty, either in food or wine or cheese, which represents the region. If one town's specialty is sausages for example, you can bet your boots it will be the best of the region, family name and pride ride on it. So we stopped at every village along the way, pedaled our bikes and loaded up with the local specialties, fresh vegetables and wine and pedaled back to our boat. Back at the boat I would drool over our purchases and start to create a meal for us based on our fresh purchases. Sometimes we didn't quiet agree on the menu, so we were obliged to consume a little more wine prior to cooking dinner to come to a consensus, it usually worked fine.

Halfway through our trip my friend, Tom, surprised me by saying he had booked us at a local restaurant for an evening meal. I objected strongly since we had all the best food you could buy on board, but he said he wanted me to relax, so be it! I should have known something was happening when Tom said I had to wear a tie! A tie! Are you crazy! I haven't worn a tie in years I said, and further more I didn't pack one for this trip. Well not to worry Tom happens to have two ties; you guessed it I wore a tie. Come to think of it I don't think I have worn one since. The other factor that should have prepared me for the evening was the taxi that came to pick us up at the boat.

After a twenty minute drive we arrive at this mansion, actually, it's an old château with its own vineyard, long driveway, manicured lawns, and a young gentleman dressed in black with white gloves ready to open the door of our taxi. Right at that point I got the message, here we were at Marc Meneau's, world famous 5 star Michelin restaurant, wow! This was going to cost a few pennies, thank God for American Express, because I was sure going to need it tonight for sure. The restaurant, which is called L' Esperance is located in a town called Vezelay, two hours south of Paris. In Burgundy, as a restaurant goes this is the epitome of luxury dining.

I have had the pleasure of dining in quite a few world-class restaurants, but this one is really unique. The food consisted of 14 courses over a period of six hours, all of them unique and delicate small portions, but all with incredibly complex flavour. Each of us had a waiter behind our chairs, and amazingly enough you never knew they were there, except when our glasses needed refilling or plates needed to be cleared. Dirty plates seemed to all of a sudden vanish; absolutely impeccable service. All in a beautiful ambiance that radiated class, luxury, and serenity at the same time; just amazing. The food is still in my "Brain Taste", I don't think that any other meal could compete with this experience; that was the consensus from our table.

At the end of the meal I asked one of our waiters if Mr. Meneau spent much time at the restaurant, since there were 17 staff: Chef, sous-Chef, prep cooks, helpers, etc. working in the kitchen. Well you should have seen the indignant look I got as a reply, followed by "This restaurant does not operate unless Mr. Meneau is personally working in the kitchen; no dish leaves the kitchen without Mr. Meneau signing off on it!" Well OK then! I got the message loud and clear. So could you please ask Mr. Meneau if we could have the pleasure of meeting him, I have come all the way from Canada to eat at his restaurant! "I'll see what I can do" was his reply.

Ten minutes or so later dressed in white with his Chef's toque a statuesque elegant man appeared, and after a brief formal greeting we all started to relax and exchange some of our professional views. I was amazed at how frank he was with me, telling me that he had no formal Chef's training but just the love and respect for food. Well a 5 star Michelin rating does not come by being sloppy in the kitchen, so my respect for this man went up by several notches.

We all found him to be so sincere, humble and accommodating, maybe the fact that he bought us two bottles of Cristal Champagne after diner helped our professional opinion of this great man. The truth be told, I'll never forget the experience of dining at L'Esperance and neither will my company. So if ever you're around Vezelay, I highly recommend you drop in, by the way you need a six month advance reservation and a credit card that can handle three zeros after the first number, but again well worth it, no regrets. Needless to say we all came back from this trip with a few extra pounds or maybe it was kilos? Whatever, a great experience.

In all fairness to the restaurant industry, credit must be given where credit is due. My first few years in Canada from a culinary point of view were rather disappointing. In Winnipeg, where I lived for 15 years, dining choices at the time were prime rib, BBQ ribs, and a form of fried chicken, vegetables that were grey, from being over cooked, and gravy, made from salt and God knows whatever else, on everything. It didn't take long before we saw a radical change to the way food was being prepared. The influence of the Asian immigrants showed us that vegetables taste better if undercooked and crisp. The Italians gave us sauces that had flavours of fresh herbs. The Greeks taught us to enjoy goat cheese and lamb and to break plates after a meal? The French well they made sure the liquor store had enough wine to satisfy them. And so the trends started to change, people went out to enjoy dining, not to simply eat because it was suppertime.

In our early years of operation in our restaurant, I recall customers asking for their Châteaubriand well done, even to the stage that I would call it burnt. But amazingly five years later the same customers ordered their "Château" medium rare or even rare, so things did change in the food industry rather quickly because of the influence of immigrants. Today all major cities in Canada offer a tremendous variety of ethnic restaurants with high standards and quality, and as result food stores are now obliged to carry ethnic foods from all over the world to satisfy the demand. We benefit from this; we no longer have the excuse of not having the proper ingredients for being able to prepare quality tasty meals.

In 1984, while in Madrid Spain to receive an International Culinary award for our restaurant, I had the pleasure to dine at another world famous restaurant called Zalacain. A fellow Chef had told me, that while in Madrid I must dine at Zalacain, so I called to make a reservation and was told that they were fully booked for the next three months. I persisted and explained my reason for being in Madrid, I was put on hold for a couple of minutes and then told that if we were to come at 9pm three days from now that they would accommodate us. I couldn't argue with that.

The day came and we were so excited to get there. We took a cab and went to the front door only to find it locked. What's going on! I knocked hard several times on the front door, checked my watch, 8:45 pm, so we were not late! Finally someone opened the door for us, welcomed us in, and sat us at our table. We looked around, not another soul in the place. I started to get concerned, when a waiter came around to our table and asked what we would like to drink, so we ordered. He presented us with the menu which was all in Spanish, so needless to say with my poor command of the language and the menu looking more like a book than a menu, I really had to really concentrate. I picked a starter, lobster bisque with black truffles, and told the waiter that I would leave the rest of the meal to the discretion of the Chef. I explained that being a Chef myself I felt that by the look of his menu I could trust him. At first blush the waiter seemed rather concerned, but he came back a few minutes later and told me that the Chef would be honored to cook for me at his discretion.

Zalacain opened in 1973 and is still going strong from what I have read. The owner, Benjamin Urdiain, designed his restaurant with "class" in mind. Decorated with textile coverings and expensive paintings on the walls, exquisite tableware and crystal glasses, and Old World etiquette. Basque and French traditional haute cuisine, rich creamy sauces, and wine reductions inspired the food. He also was responsible for the introduction of "Nouvelle Cuisine " in Spain so his menu became fusion cuisine. The restaurant boasts a wine cellar stock of 35,000 bottles, with 800 varieties from all over the world, rather impressive! Not to mention costly to maintain. His staff was comprised of 15 Chefs, plus 8 assistants, 20 waiters, and 3 valet parking attendants. Zalacain caters to celebrities, royalty, and anybody else who has money; yes, it's not cheap. In other words he caters to the "rich and famous"; entrees start at 90 euros, that's about 120 dollars in today's market.

By 1:30 am my stomach was saying, "that's enough!" So I asked for the bill, the waiter came back and asked if I would like to meet the Chef in the kitchen. "Well of course!" I replied with enthusiasm. We proceeded to the kitchen and I was introduced to the Chef and again in my poor Spanish I was trying to converse with this Chef who doesn't speak a word of English past, Hello! After about 5 minutes of this frustrating conversation I detected a slight accent, French maybe? I asked him where do you come from, he told me Brittany France, well need I say more, he came from a town 12 km from where I was born.

What a small world, now we could really converse. Half an hour later I realized that my partner was still in the dining room by herself, I think I am in trouble! So the Chef and I went back to the dining room and continued our conversation with my partner's presence, which didn't help much because she doesn't speak French. To ease the pain my new found Chef friend ordered a bottle of Spanish Champagne to celebrate our mutual motherland connection. Soon after the owner, Benjamin, showed up at our table and congratulates us on winning the culinary award and offers to treat us to a fine Cognac, Louis XIV, no less. I should have known to stop at one, but when you talk shop, one has the tendency to get carried away, so I lost count of just how many Cognacs! But let's say that the next day was spent in the hotel room, drapes closed with no chambermaid service required and gallons of aqua.

When the time came to pay, I presented my American Express card, without looking at the actual cost and told the waiter to add a 20% gratuity. It was only the next day that upon looking at my receipt that I noticed something was wrong, how could the bill be so small!!! I did the money conversion several times to make sure I hadn't screwed up, after all I was slightly inebriated last night. I called the receptionist at the restaurant and asked her to verify my bill; she came back and said it was right. When I suggested that was impossible, she advised me that Benjamin the owner had picked up the tab, except for the one starter and one bottle of wine, and said he hoped we would be back in Spain soon and wished us well on our trip home. At that point I reaffirmed my invitation of last night for him to visit with us if he ever came to Canada.

While in Madrid. I dined at another restaurant that sticks in my mind it's called La Dorada and they specialize in seafood. All the seafood is displayed on a marble counter full of chipped ice, so you basically see what you're getting. One dish I had there which stuck me was, steamed baby clams in wine. Now I have never seen or eaten clams so small, they were the size of my small fingernail; but amazingly plumb full of sweet delicate meat; I must have had 60-80 of those little morsels on my plate. The other specialty that they are famous for is Fritura Malaguena, which is a mixture of small fish about the size of an anchovy, coated with a spiced flour and fried in green virgin olive oil, topped with parsley and coarse salt. This is the Malaga style of cooking fish, very simple but very tasty.

All of the meals at La Dorada were very reasonable, and only seafood is served. The owner told me that each day he personally goes to the wharf at 5 am and waits for the fishing boats to come in. He has a small fleet of fishers that sell only to him and the fish has to be of the highest quality, in return he buys all of their catch year-round.

Fresh sardines is another seafood which is very traditional in Europe especially in the southern part, such as Italy, Greece, Portugal, and France. I remember when I was just an 11 year old kid with my father in the port city of Marseille, we had to go to the dock early one morning, my father said to get fresh grilled sardines for breakfast. Well my stomach at that point did a kind of flip, sardines for breakfast! I don't think so! It was barely dawn when we got to the dock and waited for the fishing boats to arrive. Suddenly a whole fleet of small fishing boats arrived at the docks, and each of them had a charcoal fire going in 20 litre metal cans with a grill on top. By this time there was a crowd of almost a hundred people around, and the air became permeated with the wonderful aroma of grilling sardines. When our turn came to be served all Dad said was "two". I guess that's all that was necessary, for the fisherman grabbed a couple of sheets of used newspaper and folded it into a cone and proceeded to pick six freshly grilled sardines which he put in this cone along with a couple wedges of fresh lemon on top.

By this time my apprehension about grilled sardines for breakfast changed to inquisitive, I guess since they smell so good, I should try them. Dad explained to me that the guts were still in and that the best way to handle that would be to snap the head off and pull and all the guts would come out, well he was right as always. I must say the first taste had me hooked on fresh grilled sardines for life. Unfortunately it was years before fresh or frozen sardines were available in Canada, now you can buy them frozen pretty well at any major food store. I introduced my grandchildren to grilled sardines a couple of summers ago at one of our BBQ dinners,

Michel Rabu

with the understanding that they didn't have to eat them if they didn't like the taste, but they should at least try, which they did. Unfortunately I didn't have enough sardines to satisfy their appetite, I must say I was surprised at just how much they enjoyed them.

Grilled Sardines

Serves 4

Ingredients:

8 frozen sardines

¼ cup olive oil

1 tablespoon coarse sea salt

Juice and zest of one lemon

1 lemon to squeeze over

¼ cup chopped parsley

Method:

1. Let your frozen sardines partially thaw, then with a very sharp paring knife, start by putting the end of the knife in the anus of the sardine and cut towards the head, open the stomach cavity and remove the guts, and cut the belly fins off. The head doesn't have to be removed before cooking.

2. Rinse the sardines well in cold water and put them in a bowl, drizzle them with olive oil, coarse sea salt and the juice and zest of one lemon, and toss to coat the sardines.

3. Let them marinate for about an hour in the fridge.

4. Make sure your BBQ is set at the hottest level.

5. Spray your BBQ with a non-stick spray, and place your sardines on the grill. Cook each side for about four minutes.

6. Plate and squeeze fresh lemon juice all over them and top with chopped parsley and enjoy a healthy appetizer.

A good dry white wine like "sauvignon blanc" will put the right touch to this meal.

Since we are on the topic of seafood, I am going to share a couple of shellfish recipes that were favorites of my customers at the restaurant.

Clams in White Wine

Serves 4

Ingredients:

4-5 lbs fresh Manila clams

2 medium onions quartered

4 garlic cloves, crushed

1 cups dry white wine

1 cup whipping cream

1 teaspoon black pepper

2 tablespoons chopped parsley

1 teaspoon thyme

Method:

1. Rinse the clams in cold water, to get rid of the sand that sometime sticks to the shells. After rinsing discard any clams that are not fully closed.

2. In a large stockpot, put the clams, onions, thyme and garlic, with the lid on at high heat cook for about 4 minutes or so shaking the pot a few times.

3. When you see the clams starting to open, add the wine and cook for a few minutes more with the lid still on until you see that all the clams have opened.

4. Add the cream, pepper and chopped parsley, shake the pot and let sit for a couple of minutes with the lid on.

5. Ladle the clams into a deep platter and pour the sauce over, leaving a couple of tablespoons of sauce in the pot, just in case some clams spat out sand, which will settle at the bottom of the pot.

Make sure you put tablespoons on the table you don't want to waste that wonderful broth. You can use this same recipe for fresh mussels.

Traditionally in France we cook our mussels as in the Clams in White Wine recipe, but I have come to enjoy my Asian version, Thai Mussels, you may want to try this sometime.

Thai Mussels

Serves 4

Ingredients:

4-5 lbs fresh mussels (beard removed)

2 medium onions, quartered

2 tablespoons sweet chili sauce

1 tablespoon green curry paste

1 tablespoon grated ginger

5-6 cloves, crushed garlic

¼ cup lime juice

1 can coconut milk (16oz)

½ cup chopped lemongrass

½ cup chopped cilantro

½ cup chopped green onions

Method:

1. Wash the mussels thoroughly in cold water, remove beards and discard any that are not fully closed.

2. In a large pot on high heat, combine coconut milk, curry paste, garlic, onion, chili sauce and ginger, stir well and cook for a minute or two.

3. Add the mussels, lemongrass and lime juice, cover and cook until mussels are all open. Shaking the pot a few times while cooking will help the mussels to open. Some of them will only open partially that's fine, be careful not to overcook them.

4. Sprinkle with the cilantro and green onions and serve.

A very simple yet very complex dish that is rich in flavours. This same recipe can also be used with manila clams.

Marinated Smoked Herring — Smoked Kippers

Serves 4

This dish has been well received by my friends, which was to my surprise. This is a very old recipe that became popular at the famous "Les Halles" market in Paris along with the onion soup. The truck drivers making their 2 am deliveries of fresh fish, produce and meat at the market needed some satisfying food that was quick and reasonably priced after having driven all night from all over France.

Ingredients:

8 smoked herring fillets

1 red onion, thinly sliced

1 cup olive oil

1 teaspoon ground pepper

4 medium potatoes

½ cup parsley, chopped

Method:

1. Peel the skin off of the herring fillets then cut them into bite-size pieces.

2. Layer the herring pieces in a dish along with the red onion.

3. Cover herring fillets with olive oil and fresh ground pepper.

4. Marinate for as little as 1 day or up to a couple of weeks refrigerated.

5. Cut potatoes into some bite-size pieces and boil, drain and put as many herrings as you wish on top, a little chopped fresh parsley that's it!

The combination of the hot potatoes and the cold herring, olive oil and onions makes this a wonderful appetizer anytime. Finding the smoked kippers (as they are called) can be a challenge in small cities, do not use the ones that are in a butter sauce, I find them too soft in texture for this dish.

When it comes to seafood, like I've said oysters have to be my favorite. When they are small, I like them served raw with a mignonette, which is simply finely chopped shallot, red wine vinegar and black pepper. Using a food processor put two whole peeled shallots along with ¼ cup of red wine vinegar, a dash of pepper and process until very fine. The idea is to top each oysters with a little of this mignonette sauce. You will most likely have sauce leftover, don't discard it, use it as a base for your next vinaigrette dressing, just add olive oil and more vinegar depending on how much you want to make. Just keep in mind the ratio of 2 parts oil to 1 part vinegar. The small amount of mignonette will add an intense shallot flavour to your dressing, a dash of salt and you're done.

Oysters Rockefeller

Serves 6 (2 oysters each)

When all I have is medium or large oysters I cook them "Oysters Rockefeller" which is one my favorites.

Ingredients:

12 shucked oysters, left in the shell

1 lbs fresh or frozen spinach

6 strips bacon cooked and chopped

4 tablespoons melted butter

4 tablespoons flour

1 cup warm milk

½ cup grated Parmesan

1 tablespoon Pernod liquor or 1 teaspoon ground anise

Pinch of thyme

½ teaspoon pepper

½ cup panko (Japanese white bread crumbs) or breadcrumbs

1 lb coarse salt*

> *This is to set the oysters on so that they don't tip over whilst cooking. Spread the coarse salt on a metal or ovenproof dish, this will also be used as the serving dish at the table.*

Method:

1. Set oven temperature @ 450°F.

2. Shuck oysters- reserving In a medium saucepan, melt butter then add flour and stir well, add warm milk while stirring.

3. As soon as it starts to boil remove from heat, add Parmesan, Pernod, thyme, pepper, and spinach (make sure the spinach has being squeezed well to remove all of the water). Add the bacon and stir the mixture well.

4. Place about a tablespoon of the mixture on the bottom of each the shell, place one oyster on top. Now cover each oyster with another tablespoon of the Rockefeller mixture (use all the mixture up).

5. Top oysters with a sprinkle of the panko crumbs.

6. Place the oysters in the shells on the salt dish and bake until lightly brown (10-12 min).

Bangkok Seafood Chowder

Serves 6

This dish is the result of true fusion cuisine, incorporating the classic and the new, with an Asian touch, that's why I called it "Bangkok Seafood Chowder". This makes a wonderful meal by itself or accompanied with jasmine rice as a side. Fresh taste is the forte of this chowder, so it is important to add the ingredients in the order as listed to ensure that the seafood will not be overcooked.

Ingredients:

½ cup peanut oil

2 lb mussels

4 tablespoons lemongrass* finely chopped* Frozen can be bought at Asian stores

2 tablespoons chopped fresh ginger

4 jalapeno chilies, seeded & sliced thin

8 cups chicken stock

3 medium onions, slivered

1 head of garlic

1 cup slivered celery

½ cup sliced thin carrots

2 tablespoons red or green curry paste

2 tins coconut milk 12/14 oz

1 lb snapper

1 lb salmon

1 lb prawns, shell removed

2 lb clams

1-2 lb halibut — allow 2-3 pieces of halibut per person cut
    into bite-size

½ cup chopped basil

1 cup chopped cilantro

1 cup fresh lime juice

2 tablespoons chopped green onions

Salt to taste

Method:

1. In a large stockpot, heat the oil.

2. Add onions, garlic, curry paste, lemon grass, celery, carrots, jalapenos, cook for 4-5 minutes stirring well, do not allow onions to brown.

3. Add chicken stock, coconut milk, lime juice and ginger, bring to a boil and simmer for 5 minutes.

4. Add halibut, salmon, and snapper, cook for 4-5 minutes at low simmer.

5. Add prawns, mussels, clams and chopped basil. Cook until clams are open. Do not over cook.

6. Once ready to serve, top with green onions.

If you are serving this chowder as a main, either a side of jasmine rice, or yellow flesh boiled potatoes goes well.

Living on Vancouver Island is really like living in paradise. The ocean and lakes are full of fresh seafood, available year round and most seafood can be personally harvested, by simply possessing a valid fishing license. The local woods also offer plenty for one to gather. Local farms for organic produce and meats are just a short distance away. And to top it off, no hustle of the big city, full of indifferent people walking by consumed by their electronic iPhone texting. Many using a language that will make our next generation unable to spell but it's all in the name of progress, so they say!

Dungeness crabs are plentiful, a boat a crab trap, some stinking meat or fish remnants, or cat food, will guarantee you Dungeness crab for dinner. And while you're at it, a prawn trap will also compliment your harvest and reward you with sweet spotted prawns that can be enjoyed by simply cooking in a frying pan with butter, garlic, and parsley. Simple yet so good.

Ginger Dungeness Crab

I created this dish when I first arrived on Vancouver Island; this dish came about because I was getting bored of eating just boiled crab with a drawn butter sauce, how capricious is that! Anyhow I am sure you'll also enjoy this dish. This dish is best cooked in a wok.

Ingredients:

1 Dungeness crab

½ cup ginger, thinly sliced

2 tablespoons chopped garlic

2 green peppers, cut into bite-size

1 red onion, slivered

¼ cup canola oil

1 cup Kikkoman soy sauce

3 tomatoes

½ cup chopped cilantro

Method:

1. Boil the crab, whole, for about 12 minutes.

2. Cool under the tap enough to be able to handle the crab.

3. Remove the back by holding onto the legs and back and pulling. Remove the lungs that are attached to the side of the body, and clean the center of the body under the tap until you are left with only white meat and shell. Now you want to separate the legs from the body, and crack them just enough so that a sauce will be able to penetrate to the meat inside the shell. Next, cut the white shell part of the body into four pieces.

4. Put the canola oil into the wok at high heat. When the oil starts to smoke, add the onion, ginger, garlic, and crab and toss a couple of times then add the soy sauce.

5. Put the lid on and cook on high for about 5 minutes tossing or stirring a couple of times in between.

6. Add the remaining ingredients except the cilantro, and with the lid on, cook for another 4-5 minutes.

7. Just before serving add the cilantro.

There is no elegant way to eat this dish, you'll use all your fingers, and do a lot of sucking, but again it's well worth the effort.

I have yet to find someone that has not raved about this dish. You could also cook spotted prawns the same way, just remove the head and split the backs of the shell, to expose the meat so that the sauce can flavour it.

Vancouver Island has in the last few years developed a farmed scallop and mussel fishery and I must say that I am very impressed with the product. Traditionally scallops and mussels came from the East Coast of Canada, but our local product is amazing. The scallops are large plump and sweet and the mussels the same. Quite honestly I can say, they are both better quality than their East Coast cousins. I believe the water quality is the reason, cold clean, well-flushed tide water, and lots of plankton to feed on.

Sashimi Style Scallops

Serves four

Here is a scallop recipe that is very simple, but must be made with fresh large Scallops.

Ingredients:

4 large scallops (allow one large scallop per person)

1 cup clarified butter

4 garlic cloves

Juice of two lemons, plus the zest of one lemon

¼ cup chopped parsley

¼ teaspoon Pernod

1 Anise bulb, sliced very thin

Pepper to taste

Method:

1. Place four plates in the oven set at @300°F for 15 minutes.

2. In a frying pan melt the butter and skim off the foam to clarify the butter.

3. Add the garlic, sliced anise, and lemon zest cook for 5 minutes at a low temperature. Do not allow the butter to change color.

4. Slice the scallops as thinly as possible.

5. Remove plates from the oven (using oven gloves) and place one layer of anise on each plate filling the base of the plate, then place the sliced scallops on top of the anise.

6. Add the lemon juice, Pernod, and parsley to the butter mixture and spoon onto the scallops, and serve.

The scallops will be slightly warm, and the combination of all these flavours really makes the scallops shine. Thin sliced baguette bread is a must to dip in the sauce along with a glass of Prosecco or any other dry bubbly.

Vegetable Sides

Roasted Vegetables

This version of a roasted vegetable side dish is sure to please.

Ingredients:

¼ cup olive oil

2 red and 1 green peppers, quartered

2 carrots, slivered

1 anise bulb, sliced

6 asparagus, whole

1 red onion, slivered

2 parsnips

4 yellow flesh potatoes, cut bite-size

1 tsp herbes de Provence

Juice of one lemon juice

¼ cup chopped parsley or cilantro as a garnish option

Salt and pepper to taste

Method:

1. Set oven @ 425°F.

2. Coat the bottom of a Pyrex dish with olive oil. Place all vegetables except the peppers in dish and sprinkle with oil, herbs, lemon juice, salt and pepper.

3. Cover with foil and cook for about 25 minutes.

4. Add the peppers and cook for a further 15 minutes.

Another version is using, beets, turnips, carrots, yams, and onions.

Ginger Glazed Parsnips

Parsnip is a vegetable that is low on the popularity chart, yet it has such potential as a great tasty vegetable. One season at our restaurant my produce salesman was promoting locally grown parsnips at a very reasonable cost, I ordered the 50 lb bag, which was the only size available at that price. Now what do I do with all these parsnips? Well here is the recipe that will change the flavour perception of the lowly parsnip, and had everyone asking, "what am I eating?"

Ingredients:

2 lbs parsnips

1 cup brown sugar

4 tablespoons fresh ginger (if using dried use 1 tablespoon)

1 cup chicken stock or water

Method:

1. Peel and cut the parsnips like a French fry.

2. Cover with water and cook for 5 minutes on medium heat until tender.

3. Drain, add sugar, stock and ginger and cook until the sauce has reduced by half and the parsnips are well glazed and caramelized in color. That's it! Easy and very tasty.

Stir-Fry Vegetable Side

Serves 4

Ingredients:

½ red onion, slivered

2 carrots, sliced

1 cup mushrooms, sliced

1 cup celery, sliced

2 cups other vegetables, sliced —such as snap peas, bok choy, red peppers

1 tablespoon grated ginger

1 tablespoon finely chopped garlic

¼ cup canola oil

½ cup chicken stock

1 tablespoon light soya

½ teaspoon sesame oil

1 teaspoon cornstarch

Method:

1. In a wok on high heat, add a little canola oil, then add your slivered onion, carrots, mushrooms, and celery.

2. At this stage add ginger and garlic. Cook at while stirring or tossing for a couple of minutes.

3. Add the rest of the vegetables you have chosen along with chicken stock, soya, sesame oil and cornstarch mixed all together.

4. Cook on a high heat for just 3-4 minutes, this will keep the vegetables nice and crisp and they will retain their colour.

When doing a stir-fry remember to toss your vegetables at least 5-6 times whilst cooking, this allows for even heat through out the cooking process. If tossing the wok is not your forte, then using a spatula to stir the vegetables will do just fine. The trick is to keep the vegetables moving while cooking.

I have been very fortunate to have a family that has always enjoyed food and had a great respect for it too. Waste was not a choice in my family when it came to food. I remember as a child after the war at my grandmother's farm having soup as a meal; she would take what was left of yesterday's baked farmhouse style bread and slice pieces of it on top of the vegetable soup. The bread would absorb all of the fresh flavours of those vegetables with a slight hint of chicken fat flavour to it. Hens that stopped laying were too tough for roasting so they were eventually sacrificed for stewing and that also produced a wonderful chicken stock for soups to follow. Even the meat of those chickens, served cold was very tasty. Today's chickens wouldn't stand a chance when it comes to flavour, and it is all in the way that they were raised. At grandmother's, the chickens were free to roam and pick at whatever was around; once in a while we would take a small bucket of grain and throw it at them as a special treat. Grain was very scarce after the war, so you kept all you could to sow in your fields for the next year's crop.

Potatoes were also very precious to us, being a staple of our diet. I recall a potato taste that was unique; just before the new harvest of potatoes we would take what was left in the root cellar of last year's crop and boil them in a big copper cauldron on an open fire in the middle of the driveway at the farm. We would simmer the potatoes for hours then put them in a wheelbarrow when they were still warm and take them to the outside pig pen, where the pigs would feast. I would always take a couple of those potatoes for myself. I would put them in my pocket and proceed to the hay barn, climb on top of the bales of hay and feast on my two potatoes along with a fresh cracked egg, which the hen just laid in the haystack. Sounds nasty, but no, it was a wonderful combination of the freshest protein and starch. It must have been great if 65 years later I can still "Brain Taste" it and enjoy it! It's amazing how little things from your youth stay with you with such clarity and bring joy all over again.

Pomme de Terre Boulangiere

Serves 4

Don't let the name intimidate you, in French it means "potatoes, baker's wife style", don't ask me why that's the name! But try this someday.

Ingredients:

8 medium potatoes preferably Norgold or Yukon gold variety

3 large onions

2 cups chicken stock

1 cup cheese, Swiss or mozzarella

1 pinch of nutmeg

1 tablespoon chopped rosemary

You should not need salt since there is some already in the stock & the cheese

Method:

1. Butter the sides and bottom of an 8"x10 "or a 9"x12" baking dish.
2. Slice potatoes like for a scalloped potato.
3. Slice the onions.
4. Arrange one layer of potatoes on the bottom of pan.
5. Place a layer of sliced onions over the potato layer.
6. Repeat this process until all potatoes and onions are used up.
7. Cover the potatoes and onions with chicken stock and sprinkle the chopped rosemary and nutmeg over the top.
8. Top with grated Swiss or mozzarella cheese and ground pepper.

9. Bake @ 375°F for 40 minutes or until golden brown, and all the liquid is absorbed. Now you'll see what chicken stock does for plain scallop potatoes.

This is a nice complimentary side to a roast leg of lamb Provencal

I am glad to see the trend towards shopping locally: farmers market popularity, people's concern about healthy living and even in some cities new bylaws allowing for the raising of chickens for personal egg production. All of this tells me that some people are genuinely concerned about what they eat and so they should be.

I talk to people that have for the first time in their lives started growing some vegetables or herbs in their backyard in pots or raised bed. Nothing big, but it's a start. After their first crop harvest they all say the same thing, next year I am going to grow more, because of the joy and satisfaction that they had with their first encounter with gardening.

Salads & Dressings

French people don't make a lot of different salads, usually a green salad: no iceberg lettuce, with a plain vinaigrette is the norm. Except in the south of France where Salade Nicoise for lunch is traditional, mainly because of the warmer weather, and not wanting to spend too much time in a hot kitchen cooking, so greens and proteins all cold and on one plate makes sense.

In French cuisine, a green salad with a meal is usually consumed after the main course with the belief that this will cleanse you palate and help with digestion. I guess there is some validity to that belief. Salads are often also made for a nice clean taste preamble to the traditional cheese platter.

One area where you can save a substantial amount of money is by making your own salad dressings and trust me it's so easy. The basic rule is one part acid to two or three parts oil. Two parts oil when using mild vinegar like cherry vinegar or rice vinegar, three parts when you are using balsamic or regular vinegar. The rest of the ingredients usually include mustard or egg yolk, which act as a binder to thicken the dressing, the rest is up to your imagination and taste, let's try a few recipes.

French Mayonnaise

Yields 2 cups

If you have a blender or food processor, you can make 2 cups of mayonnaise in less than a minute. Egg yolks, mustard, lemon juice, blend, then add the oil in a steady stream until all the oil is used, add salt and pepper to taste and you're done, and half the cost of store bought and no added chemicals.

Ingredients:

3 egg yolks at room temperature

1 tablespoon Dijon mustard

1 tablespoon lemon juice

2 cups canola oil*

Salt and pepper to taste

For a richer taste use olive oil instead of canola or for lighter taste use grape seed oil.

Method:

1. In a bowl, combine egg yolks at room temperature, Dijon mustard, lemon juice and blend with a hand blender, or a hand mixer for 1minute.

2. Drizzle in about 1 cup of canola oil while continuing to blend with the blender, keep adding more canola oil until you have a firm consistency to your mayo.

3. Add salt and pepper to taste.

4. Balance the mayo to your taste by adding more lemon juice and that's it.

Stores in fridge for up to three weeks

Thousand Island Dressing

Yields 3.75 cups

This recipe uses your French mayo as a base.

Ingredients:

- ¼ cup finely chopped onion (½ medium onion)
- ½ cup dill relish
- 1 tablespoon Worcestershire
- 1 cup ketchup
- 1 teaspoon Tabasco
- 2 cups homemade French mayo

Method:

1. Combine all ingredients and process until smooth with a hand blender.

Stores for up to three weeks in the fridge if using fresh mayo.

Caesar Salad Dressing

Yields 3 cups

This Caesar dressing can also be used as a marinade for chicken breast, pork chops, and even fish like halibut or snapper. Marinate for a couple of hours and coat with panko, Japanese breadcrumbs that stay nice and crisp and light.

Ingredients:

- 2 heads of garlic
- 1 small tin of anchovies

2 tablespoons capers

1 tablespoon Tabasco

2 tablespoons Worcestershire

½ cup lemon juice

2 cups homemade French mayo

Method:

2. In the food processor, combine all ingredients except mayo and process until smooth.

3. Add the mayo and process for another minute.

4. Taste by dipping a piece of bread in the dressing, this will tell you if the dressing is balanced to your liking. You may want to adjust accordingly with more lemon juice, or pepper.

This dressing will keep refrigerated for a couple of months.

As you can see, we do not use water or thickeners like most commercial dressings do. Check it out next time you are shopping and you'll notice that the first ingredient is often water, then a whole bunch of chemicals you can't pronounce, that can't be good for you!

Our restaurant became quite famous for its Caesar salad. Our waiters made them at the table, I can remember on some nights they would make as many as twenty of these each; that's 80-90 salads a day. It was quite a show and each waiter had his own little touch that differed from the other waiters, maybe it was more garlic, or less anchovies, or more Parmesan, whatever the customers wanted. After the restaurant had made 30 thousand Caesar salads over the years, we stopped counting. To this day we still have people asking for it.

Assembling a Caesar Salad

Start with heads of fresh romaine preferably from a local farm, break apart the romaine into bite-size pieces into a bowl, add bacon bits*, croutons, chopped green onions, and freshly grated or shaved Parmesan Regiano. Toss, then add your dressing and toss again. Serve onto chilled plates.

*Making your own bacon bits is easy, especially if you have food processor. Cook 1 lb of lean bacon until crisp, cool then put into a food processor and pulse until you have the bacon bits of size you want. These freeze very well.

Croutons

Making your own croutons is also easy and better tasting than any store bought one. Every year I get called upon to cook a large family turkey dinner and I usually make my own croutons for the stuffing from multi grain baguettes. This one time I felt lazy and decided to buy the croutons for the stuffing, well did I get a shock at the checkout $13.00 a kilo for croutons full of MSG and who knows what else. I can make my own healthy croutons for less than half the price; needless to say I have never again bought readymade croutons and my family and friends just love my stuffing.

Ingredients:

1 rustic, multigrain bread loaf

1 tablespoon Italian spice mix

4 tablespoons olive oil

Method:

1. Preheat oven to 375°F.

2. Cut bread into approximately ½-inch squares.

3. Put bread cubes, Italian spice mix and olive oil into a plastic storage/ freezer bag and toss vigorously.

4. Spread bread on a cookie sheet and bake until dry and crisp, approximately 10 minutes.

5. Cool and freeze any extras that will not be used right away.

Tip: At your supermarket they have day old bread at half price on a regular basis; buy two or three loaves of rustic, or French baguettes, follow the above method, and there you have croutons, no chemicals, or additives.

You can also convert your croutons to a great tasting seasoned breading by simply processing hem with a little Parmesan, parsley, and garlic (optional) to a very fine crumb. This beats Shake & Bake in a taste test anytime and costs at least half the price. Once the crumbs are made they can be frozen. I'll usually make two batches of breadcrumbs —one coarse to use on roasts, and chops, and the other super fine, to use for coating fish, chicken breast, or schnitzels.

Braised Radicchio

4 side servings

Braised radicchio lettuce is one of my favorite salads during the summer and fall when this lettuce is available from the local farmers market. This recipe is not French but Italian, mainly from the Tuscany region, although it's become rather fashionable in the south of France as of late.

Ingredients:

1 head radicchio lettuce

DRESSING:

3 tablespoons extra virgin olive oil

1 tablespoon aged balsamic vinegar

4 garlic cloves, crushed

4 anchovies fillets, chopped fine

Pepper to taste

Zest of one lemon

2 tablespoons chopped fresh basil

*Option * You may use your homemade Caesar dressing*

Method:

1. Cut the radicchio into four sections (wedges). Do not cut out the core.

2. Mix all dressing ingredients together.

3. Coat all pieces of radicchio with dressing and let sit for ½ hour.

4. Continue using the BBQ method or the oven method as below.

BBQ METHOD:

Place radicchio on hot grill and cook each side for 3 minutes. Remove the core and plate spreading the leaves. Mix pepper and lemon with basil sprinkle over and serve. If you have a little dressing left over pour it over the lettuce.

OVEN METHOD:

Place radicchio on a baking sheet @400°F and follow same method as for the BBQ recipe.

Leek and Orange Salad

Serves 4 as a side

Another summer salad that I am very fond of is this leek and orange salad. This is a great refreshing and different tasting salad that can be used instead of an appetizer. I find that steaming the white part of the leeks the day before and refrigerating over night keeps the leeks firm and easier to slice.

Ingredients:

6 fresh leeks

3 oranges, segmented

Organic arugula or baby mixed greens

Basil or parsley

DRESSING:

1 shallot

⅔ cup grape seed oil

⅓ cup orange juice

1 tablespoon frozen orange juice

1 teaspoon Dijon mustard

2 teaspoons honey

Salt and pepper to taste

Method:

1. Cut and retain only the white part of the leeks (freeze and save the green tops for chicken stock).

2. Steam for 5 minutes, you don't want them soft or mushy. Then cool in fridge.

3. Cut your orange into segments removing any white skin, (option you can use a can of mandarin oranges).

4. In a food processor mix all the dressing ingredients, adding the oil last in a steady stream while the machine is working, this will ensure a smooth dressing.

5. Slice your leeks 1" thick cut on a diagonal.

6. Combine orange segments and leeks.

7. Place leeks and oranges on a bed of organic arugula or baby mixed greens, and drizzle with the dressing then top with fresh chopped parsley or basil.

I like to keep the leeks and oranges in the fridge until ready to serve, and have the plates chilled before plating. Shaved Parmesan Reggiano or goat cheese along with sliced avocado is a nice over the top version of this refreshing summer salad.

Tomato & Bocconcini Salad a.k.a. Caprese Salad

Serves 4 as an appetizer or side

One more salad that I enjoy is a Tomato Bocconcini salad but only in August. This is when the local heirloom tomatoes are available at the farmers market and the cheese is fresh and I have lots of wonderful organic basil at my disposal, so this is what I do with all this

Ingredients:

4 large organic tomatoes, preferably heirloom type*

3 large balls of fresh Bocconcini cheese

¼ cup chopped fresh basil

> *Heirloom tomatoes are usually uneven in shape or size but will reward you with the real taste of tomatoes of the past, as they should be.*

DRESSING:

2 garlic cloves, chopped fine

3 tablespoons extra virgin olive oil

2 tablespoons old balsamic vinegar

Salt and pepper to taste

Method:

1. Slice the tomatoes and the cheese ¼ " thick.

2. On a platter arrange one slice of tomato, next a slice of cheese behind the tomato slice and continue this process until all the cheese and tomatoes are used.

3. Mix all the ingredients for making the dressing.

4. Pour the dressing over the cheese and tomatoes and sprinkle the fresh chopped basil over the salad and serve.

If you are using a regular balsamic vinegar and you want to enhance the quality and flavour, simmer any amount of balsamic until it has reduced by half, it will thicken and become a syrup with lots of sweet flavour. As a matter of fact if you have never tried strawberries and reduced balsamic vinegar you are missing out on a great summer dessert.

Variations in presentation of caprese salad

Desserts

Desserts are not something that I spend a lot of time doing. I enjoy a cheese and fruit platter after dinner with a nice wine and maybe a little Cognac. My family often requests certain desserts that they enjoy, one of them is a Grand Marnier cheesecake, and I must admit that whenever I make one I also enjoy it.

Grand Marnier Cheesecake

Serves 14 adults

For years this was a trademark dessert at our restaurant so I guess I should share this recipe with you.

Ingredients:

1.5 kilo cream cheese

12 oz sugar

12cz can mandarin oranges, drained

8 eggs

4 oz Grand Marnier (or Cointreau)

3 cups graham cracker crumbs

1 cup brown sugar

½ cup soft butter (or margarine)

Method:

1. Set oven @325°F.

2. Mix all crust ingredients together and spread into a 9-10" spring form pan.

3. Press evenly using a spatula, and bake for 10 minutes. Then set aside to cool.

4. Reduce oven temperature to 300°F.

5. In a food processor, combine the cream cheese cut into small chunks; mandarin oranges, eggs, sugar, and Grand Marnier, process until the mixture is very smooth. You may have to scrape the sides of the processor a couple of times to achieve this.

6. Once the mixture is smooth pour into the crust and bake @300°F for one hour to one and a half hours depending on your oven. The center should be firm but not split.

7. Let the cake cool overnight in the refrigerator.

A raspberry coulis or a chocolate sauce is a nice compliment to the cheesecake. A warning this cheesecake is very rich, so small wedge portions are recommended. This cake will serve 14 adults and it keeps well in the fridge for up to a week, that is if you can resist the temptation of that midnight snack!

I have friends and some members of my family that are lactose intolerant so when cooking for them I have to restrain my French training for butter and whipping cream, and substitute with Soy or coconut milk, which by the way work quite well. I use cornstarch if I need to thicken the dish or sauce instead of the traditional roux. Here is a dessert that I have found, it's simple and quick and a very rich dessert for chocolate lovers that are lactose intolerant.

Chocolate Mousse (lactose free)

Serves 4

Ingredients:

2 cups silk tofu (no substitute)

6 oz dark chocolate 70% cocoa or more

¼ cup sugar

2 oz Grand Marnier or Cointreau

1 small basket fresh raspberries (or frozen whole berries)

Method:

1. In a double boiler melt the chocolate, cool to 90°F.

2. Put the Silk Tofu and sugar in a food processor and blend until smooth.

3. Slowly add the melted chocolate, when well blended add the Grand Marnier.

4. Pour mixture into wine glasses, cover and chill for at least one hour.

5. Top with berries before serving.

Seasonal fresh fruits with yogurt ice cream are also another quick dessert for lactose intolerant guests.

CAUTION:

Yogurt contains live bacterial cultures that when it enters the intestine it converts to lactic acid; which is why one can tolerate this lactose product. On the other hand frozen yogurt does not contain live bacterial cultures, so one may show signs of intolerance when eating yogurt ice cream and no signs when eating live yogurt.

Pavlova

4 servings

When it comes to desserts I have few favourites. When I was in Australia I was introduced to the most famous Aussie dessert Pavlova named after Anna Pavlova, the great Russian ballerina who came to perform there, what I like is it's light, very easy to make as well as reasonable. I make meringue shells whenever I have frozen or fresh egg whites that need to be used. Once made the shells will keep for months stored in a metal or plastic air-tight box in the pantry and can be a quick impromptu dessert if you have fruit and whipping cream on hand.

Ingredients:

4 egg whites

1-½ cups sugar

1 teaspoon vanilla

1 teaspoon lemon juice

2 teaspoons cornstarch

For each individual pavlova ½ cup sliced fresh fruit and ¼
   whipped cream

   *for a richer flavour add a ¼ cup of mascarpone cheese to the whipped cream

Method:

1.   Set oven to 300°F.

2.   In a mixer whip, egg whites, sugar and vanilla to firm stage.

3.   Add lemon juice and cornstarch.

4.   The base is easy to make; you want to pipe the egg mixture on a parchment lined cookie sheet making a circle of about 4 inches. Then pipe a layer around the edge, and add another layer on top, so what you have is a circle with a two layer wall like a bird's nest.

5.   Bake for one hour and then let rest on a wire rack in a dry area (very important).

6.   Mix the fruit and whipping cream together and scoop the mixture onto each meringue. Top with chopped fresh mint.

Rum Soaked Chocolate Bread Pudding

8-10 individual Ramekin size portions

This dessert is great to make because you can make several portions and freeze them to use at a later date. It's also inexpensive and for chocolate lovers this is a real treat.

Ingredients:

2 par-baked French baguettes

3 cups milk

1 cup whipping cream

1 cup sugar

1 cup brown sugar

1 tablespoon vanilla

6 eggs, beaten

20-oz dark chocolate chunks

1 cup dark rum or chocolate liqueur

1 cup crushed almonds or dried or frozen cranberries (optional)

Method:

1. Set oven @ 350°F.

2. Butter and flour 8-10 ramekins, set aside.

3. Cut baguettes into small bite-size chunks and put in a large mixing bowl along with almonds or cranberries.

4. Bring the milk, whipping cream, vanilla, and sugar to almost the boil stage in a saucepan over medium, add the chocolate and stir until dissolved, stirring constantly. Remove from heat.

5. Add the beaten eggs to the chocolate mixture and mix well, then add in the rum.

6. Add the chocolate mixture to the bread chunks and mix until the bread is coated with the chocolate mixture. Let sit for 10 minutes.

7. Stir the mixture then fill each ramekin to the top. Place ramekins in a water bath, ⅔rd to the top of the dishes. Cover with aluminum foil. Bake for 1 hour.

8. Serve immediately.

Before serving, I like to warm them in the microwave for a couple of minutes, then unmold them onto a plate and drizzle a teaspoon or so of rum onto the center of the pudding. I then drizzle a cold raspberry coulis* all over and if you want to take it a notch over the top, fresh whipped cream does the trick.

Any unused pudding, simply cover with a plastic film and put in a plastic storage/ freezer bag and freeze for a later date. To serve from frozen just microwave for 3 minutes.

*Raspberry coulis or any berry coulis is simply 1 cup of fresh or frozen fruit blended in a food processor, strained then blended with ½ cup simple syrup (dissolve ½ cup sugar into ½ cup boiling water then add 1 teaspoon of diluted cornstarch and mix well and let cool).

Fresh Strawberries with Balsamic Vinegar

Fresh strawberries, washed and cut into quarters, topped with a balsamic vinegar reduction then served with strawberry yogurt ice cream, topped with fresh chopped mint. Now what could be more simple than that, and so summery and fresh tasting.

Balsamic Reduction

The idea in making a balsamic reduction is to convert inexpensive non-aged balsamic vinegar into a sweet, full flavoured syrup.

One bottle of any balsamic vinegar slowly simmered until it becomes like corn syrup in texture, this can take 30-60 minutes to achieve. This reduction will last a very longtime in the refrigerator, and can be used on top of salads, meats, fish, and fresh fruits especially strawberries.

Fresh Strawberries with Balsamic Vinegar

My grandmother's farm in Brittany, France had an orchard, which produced some of the best apples I have ever tasted. Sweet and crunchy, almost with pink meat inside, those were my favourite eating apple. There were a couple of older trees that produced large, green, tart and very firm apples and there was no way you'd want to bite into one of those; I tried once and my lips stayed puckers for what seemed like hours later!

Grandma used the tart apples for baking on the ashes of the open-hearth fireplace. She would core them, stuff them with sweet fresh farm butter, brown sugar and crushed hazelnuts, and top them with more of the fresh hazelnuts that were picked from our trees. The dish the apples were cooked in was placed directly on the ashes near the fire and after an hour or so the apple skins were wrinkled and brown from the butter and sugars caramelizing. The bottom of the pan had a wonderful natural juice that we would spoon on top of the cooked apples. These apples had so much natural pectin that the juice in that pan would solidify into a jelly when it cooled down. Of course I would volunteer to do the dishes, so that I could lick that wonderful jelly, talk about "Brain Taste". Soft inside and sweet, I can taste them as if it were yesterday, so simple, but so good, and healthy.

The satisfaction of harvesting is the most fulfilling reward one can have; there is no money that can buy that experience. I feel sorry for people that have always lived in the city, never having experienced the farm life where everything you eat is from your soil and labor and the yield and taste depends on how well you managed your crop or animals. I remember seeing children's amazed looks when they came on a farm tour and I would take them to the greenhouse and let them taste yellow cherry tomatoes right off the vine. Many of them would say "I don't like tomatoes", so I would coax them into trying by telling them that they were like candy, they would try and then they wanted more. What amazed me the most was the lack of basic knowledge about growing food: how the plants grew, what you do to make them grow, how you harvested the produce, etc. It's not that they weren't interested; it's just that they had never been exposed to it. Many of these children came back to the farm several times a year to visit, and the parents would say that the children had learnt so much on their visits; as a result we started a day camp during the summer for children, which became very popular. We would make them participate with us in the morning and afternoon chores, of the feeding of the animals, harvesting produce, and teaching them the basics of farm life. Most of these children came back year after year, much to their parent's amazement.

We know that children seem to have a natural distaste for vegetables, so once in a while we would teach the children to make pizza dough and then we would harvest fresh vegetables in the garden: tomatoes, broccoli, spinach, cauliflower, and basil, these are not kids' favourites. Despite the children's apparent dislike of the pizza toppings, by the time they made their own personal pizzas with these vegetables and cooked them, there would be nothing left on the plates. I am sure we could have fed them these types of pizzas all week long. Parents would tell me how surprised they were to find their children all of a sudden eating, broccoli, tomatoes etc. Which I guess point to the fact that fresh is tastier and even children can tell the difference.

Eat From the Earth, Not the Box

The following food analysis warrants concerns if we are going to be responsible parents. These numbers tell me that I should NOT feed these to my children, nor should I eat them myself on a regular basis either.

- A&W - 3 chicken strips with regular fries: 710 Calories - 32gm Fat - 1840mg Sodium.
- Tim Hortons — Chili (large): 410 Calories - 22gm Fat - 1530mg Sodium.
- Hamburger Helper with cheese shells: 959 Calories - 48gm Fat - 1757mg Sodium.
- McCain three cheese pizza pockets: 500 Calories - 37gm Fat - 625mg Sodium
- McDonald quarter pounder: 530 Calories - 41gm fat - 1100mg Sodium
- Schneider's Lunchables (bologna): 390 Calories - 23gm Fat - 400mg Sodium
- Processed cheese (one slice 21gm): 300mg Sodium vs. Swiss cheese slice 28gm - 73mg Sodium

When you consider that the Canadian health food guide recommends a maximum sodium intake of 1200mg per day for a child of 4-8 years old and 1500mg for adults, the above examples should trigger the alarm bell. Consuming that amount of FAT and SODIUM on a regular basis will put you at risk of either obesity, high blood pressure, diabetes or all of the above. Your child going to school with their Lunchables has no idea of what you are doing to their health. Good healthy homemade lunches take very little time to prepare and they will save you money and protect your health.

Sugar the silent killer! According to Dr. Lewis Cantley, head of cancer research, N.Y. Weill Cornell Medical Centre, sugars are associated with obesity, heart disease and type 2 diabetes. The average Canadian consumes an average of 26 teaspoons of sugar a day (when all you need is 9 teaspoons for men and 6 teaspoons for women), that's 40 kilograms of sugar a year. One 355ml can of cola contains 40 gram or 10 teaspoons of sugar!

The food industry, when designing new products, adds sugar and salt so as to achieve what they call "the bliss factor". "The bliss factor" is when we are satisfied with the sugar or salt content of the product, one could also call it ADDICTION; we do not need anywhere the amount of salt or sugar that processed foods put in their products. Addiction creates REPEAT SALES, we get conditioned to the taste, alcoholics have the same problem. Remember when tobacco companies back in the 60's promoted their products? Movie stars, athletes, and beautiful women all showing smoking as the "normal healthy thing to do" and look at it now. Maybe we need to put the same pressure on food companies, after all it affects our health. It's not a matter of choice, we all have to eat, they should have a moral, social responsibility to produce healthy food and the government should legislate, sugar, salt, fat contents of all processed food. Their motivation should be to maintain a sustainable health care system, and a healthy productive society.

From 1960 to 2010, Dr. Robert Lustig's studies have found that the rate increase for heart disease, obesity, cancer and Type 2 diabetes has grown at the same relative ratio as the consumption of SUGAR increases. I am NOT a scientist, but the above correlation has me thinking…

Food labels for a product will read what it contains: sugar, corn syrup, fructose, white grape juice, barley malt, invert sugars… What they are NOT telling you is that all of these are SUGAR.

If you have a weight problem the best diet is based on fresh vegetables and proteins, no processed foods, and most of all SMALLER portions, and of course no snacking after or in between meals, unless it's fruits. Also a full healthy breakfast, a light lunch, and a balanced dinner, with no pop or sodas. Remember that if you train your stomach to consume large amounts of food on a regular basis, your stomach will enlarge itself to accommodate that volume of food. Then when it's not full it will tell you to eat more, as a result you'll never lose weight, that's why doctors recommend stomach restriction surgery for very obese people. Exercise is also very important, but I personally prefer a steady daily active routine, rather than going to the gym and pushing it to the limits for an hour or so. To me that seems dangerous, it's like driving a car flat out for an hour verses driving it a steady speed for 8 hours, flat out is more likely to cause breakdowns more often. I believe the human body operates in a similar way, as a matter of fact most people that live to be a hundred or more seem to have a common denominators "steady paced lifestyles" which is usually linked to their ethnic moray's and diets. Japanese, Chinese, Mediterranean, and Northern European... global disease data seems to correlate with this theory.

I am very concerned about the state of health of our society today. One in four is considered overweight, and we are ingesting to many chemicals that are infused into processed foods: chlorine, MSG, color, aspartame, disodium phosphate, EDTA, calcium chloride, sodium, tripotassium phosphate, diglycerides, sulphur dioxide, fluoride, and the list goes on. Surely these cannot be good for your system, so knowing what you're eating and where it came from is more important today than ever before. This means staying away from processed foods as much as possible, not only will you be saving money, you'll be eating healthier. Eating lots of fresh vegetables and locally produced organic food is the answer.

More and more recent studies recommend to "Eat Organic", especially when it comes to vegetables. The US Department of Agriculture and Food and Drug administration has produced a list of 53 fruits and vegetables that have a high pesticide residue. I will list the first twelve on that list, this may surprise you because we have all being taught that these twelve fruits and vegetables are "good for you". Now the lower the number, the higher the pesticide residue.

1. Apples
2. Celery
3. Strawberries
4. Peaches
5. Spinach
6. Nectarines
7. Grapes
8. Bell Peppers
9. Potatoes
10. Blueberries
11. Lettuce
12. Kale/ Collard Greens

I am sure you're as surprised as I was, so the recommendation is to buy these ORGANIC whenever you can.

On the other hand the following twelve are considered "clean" in comparison.

1. Onions
2. Corn
3. Pineapples
4. Avocado
5. Asparagus
6. Sweet Peas
7. Mangoes
8. Eggplant
9. Cantaloupe
10. Kiwi
11. Cabbage
12. Watermelon

Corn on this list concerns me because corn was one of the first crops to be genetically modified organism, GMO. That's why they require little pesticide, but do we know what GMO crops will do to our system, or what effect it will have on the future generations? The answer is a resounding "NO", so do we want to gamble with our health or that of our children!

2500 years ago, Hippocrates said "Let your food be your medicine, and your medicine be your food", I feel this should be our mantra for a long healthy life. There is strong evidence that substances used in pest control are harming humans, wildlife, and the environment. Unfortunately, Canada has been very slow in doing anything about this problem, while the European community, New Zealand and Australia have all taken a very positive position in addressing this problem. Here is a list of chemicals "approved for use" in Canada to this day, yet banned in the above countries since early 2000.

ATRAZINE:

Used in corn production.
Concerns: ground water contamination.

CARBARYL:

Used in the production of 40 pesticides.
Concerns: potential carcinogen for animals.

LINURON:

Found in eight pesticide products approved for agriculture in Canada.
Concerns: malformation in male reproductive organs.

TRILURALIN:

Top selling herbicides used in the prairie provinces. Banned in Europe. Concerns: toxic to fish, and its ability to travel by air.

This is only a small list of some of the most common pesticides used in Canada that should be banned because of potential health issues.

Maybe we need to think about this:

PESTICIDES — HERBICIDES — FUNGICIDES:
Could this eventually lead to GENOCIDE?

It seems that allergies are a very common phenomenon these days. Right from an early age we have children with all types of allergies. On top of the list is peanut allergy, coincidentally peanuts was one of the first GMO crops, next was corn. The latest report from the USA is that 70% of all processed foods contain GMO altered foods and/or HFCS, high fructose corn syrup, which is a sweetener, derived from corn. Could there be a relationship with the rise in allergy and GMO altered foods?

Reading food labels is very important, especially these days when manufacturers try to circumvent the law. Chicken and beef stocks are very popular, unfortunately most of them use words like chicken stock concentrate, or beef stock concentrate on their labels, which means that they used chemically processed flavours and extracts to simulate a chicken or beef like flavour. In the chicken, for example, the only part of real chicken in there is "fat". As for the beef, caramel becomes the flavour stimulant in the mix, MSG, sodium, artificial colors, whey, milk solids are also used, and as a result most "stocks" contain half of your daily limit of sodium. Some products list No MSG added on their labels, but they fail to tell you that the concentrates they use already have MSG, but they didn't add it someone else did. This is not recommended for people with high blood pressure, or any illness that requires a low sodium diet. The solution is to make your own, it's easy and healthy. You can control what goes in that stock.

Developing countries that have embraced the fast food fad are showing the consequences after one generation. Obesity is becoming rampant along with a major increase in premature type two diabetes; the question you have to ask yourself is "is the convenience of processed and fast foods worth the health risk?" I have become obsessed with food labels and each time I read one I just shudder, especially when I see shoppers whose carts are full of convenient processed food. In cases where children, in an age group of five to fourteen years old or so, are shopping with their parent inevitably the majority is overweight. This is sad because the kids don't know the health consequences of what they are being fed and also makes them addicted to the high sodium contents of those foods. Parents must be accountable for their children's health. After all parents are custodians and responsible for their' children's well being, or is this old fashion thinking!

Sitting down at the table as a family enjoying a home cooked meal and having a discussion of the day's events seems to be a thing of the past. Everyone is so busy, or should I say too busy to care. I don't want to sound like I am preaching but really we must address the problem if we want to see a generation that will appreciate life as it was meant to be, and everyone has that responsibility.

I thank my parents for having shown me the value of true family life and appreciation for fresh and quality food.

The Future of Food
Health, Your Choice!

Food availability is unfortunately taken for granted. We go to the store, fill our shopping carts and never think about where this food comes from, or how is it grown, or made, who handled it, what impact it had on the people who grew it, and in most cases we don't even look at the price. This attitude must change if we want to continue to enjoy what food availability we have.

In many parts of the world, we see a diminishing level of bees and bumblebees. As a matter of fact in some parts of China there are no bees left; all the fruit trees are hand pollinated with a feather by a human. In the USA some states show a decline of up to 87% in the bee population, Europe has also shown similar signs. The bee decline is has been found to be related mainly to pollutants, and pesticides. This should be a real wake up call to us, to be more concerned about what we buy and how it's grown and where it's from.

Developing countries that need that almighty export dollar are put under great pressure to over produce, consequently more lands are de-forested, and more fertilizers and pesticides are used. Water tables become polluted and that polluted water becomes part of the irrigation for the plants exposing our food to continuous high levels of concentrated chemicals. Cancer rates and types of cancer have soared during the last 30 years, that I can see, even pets such as dogs are now commonly dying of some form of cancer something that was almost unheard of 30 years ago. Is there a relationship?

I don't know. I am not a scientist, but common sense and research that I have done tells me that the probability of a correlation is high.

The carbon footprint factor is something that we can help reduce just by the food that we buy. For example: garlic from China, cherries from Chile in December, beans from Ghana, pears from Australia. Maybe we need to shop with the attitude of sustainability and seasonal approach rather than convenience. If not we will all pay the price for our actions with ill health, which will lead to dire consequences on our health care system and our children are the ones that have the most to lose.

Australia has the most stringent laws forbidding the use of additives, colour, MSG, and chlorine in children's food. England as well as most of the European community have now taken the same route. This is after studies have shown a correlation between attention deficit disorder and some chemicals in food and soft drinks. North America is still studying the problem.

Is it possible that large food conglomerates do not care about our health? The more additives we consume by eating most processed foods, the more likely we will pay the price with our health.

Some facts from "Global Cancer Statistics"

Regions with the HIGHEST Breast Cancer: North America

Regions with the LOWEST Breast Cancer: China, Japan, Australia, NZ

Regions with the HIGHEST Colon & Rectal Cancer: China, Central America

Regions with the LOWEST Colon & Rectal Cancer : Australia, Europe, North America, Japan

Regions with the HIGHEST Liver Cancer: Northern Europe, Australia, NZ, North America

Regions with the LOWEST Liver Cancer: China, Japan

Regions with the HIGHEST Stomach Cancer: North America, Australia, NZ

Regions with the LOWEST Stomach Cancer: Japan, China

One has to look at these statistics with caution; because they represent an average and correlate traditional eating habits and general life style. With these statistics it makes one think that the axiom "you are what you eat" is more important today than ever, I believe.

We can be instrumental to better health and longer life by starting to buy locally produced food, raised and grown by people with integrity who do not support the use of antibiotics, growth hormones or pesticides. Of course we cannot change genetic pre-disposition, but we can make a difference in our health by what and how much we eat. Actually the later is probably the biggest factor in addressing health issues like diabetes, high blood pressure and heart disease.

The high consumption of soft drinks and fast food by our younger population seems to be directly linked to the obesity problem prevalent in most developed countries that have embraced the fast food approach to eating and the "Super Sized" advertising factor that goes along with it. The first disease to manifest itself as a result in young people is premature type two diabetes, this of course leads to further medical complications later in life, which financially impact our health care system. However, we cannot just blame the fast food giants for all of these problems, after all as responsible adults we should have stopped our children from eating these meals or starting to smoke. Now we even have "high energy drinks" loaded with chemicals and caffeine levels that make the drinker addicted to the product, which is exactly what the manufacturers want, who cares about your health! Like I said, its time to re-align our lifestyle and ourselves.

We have drifted away from our traditional eating habits and the results have not been positive, so maybe it's time to re-evaluate our eating habits. This starts at the what food we buy level; when shopping start by buying proteins first, this will guide you on what vegetables to buy to compliment your meal. Remember if you're stuck as to what vegetables to buy, think vegetable stir fry" with six or seven vegetables, this is the easiest, healthiest and quickest dish to prepare and it pairs well with any protein. Or if you prefer roasted vegetables this is another easy dish with lots of flavours that pairs well with any roasted protein dish, such as chicken, beef or pork.

Gluten-free

To Be or No to Be? That is the Question

Every so often society manages to come up with a new social trend, which usually takes many years of research to condone or condemn. 2010, bought us gluten-free; it took a while but by 2015, in Canada alone sales of gluten-free grocery products hit 4 billion dollars a year and is growing by leaps and bounds.

Manufacturers are delighted with this opportunity to make an extra 15-35% more for gluten-free products than their regular versions; everybody is getting on the bandwagon. For example, check the price on regular pasta versus gluten-free pasta: 50-75% more for gluten-free.

In 2015, Health Canada reports that we have 35,000 Canadians with celiac disease yet we sell gluten-free products to 4 million Canadians. Now, this has me wanting to know — why? My research shows that word of mouth, articles printed, and TV shows are mainly responsible for the runaway trend of the gluten-free diet much like many other diets of the past. But a lot of people are saying that they feel so much better since abstaining from gluten, bloating gone, weight control better, more energy, etc... So there has to be a reason. I believe the reason is that people who want to be gluten-free are doing something that they never did before...reading processed food labels. What do they find? Well, that most processed foods contain gluten, so now they don't buy processed foods for this reason alone.

Results of cutting out gluten: Bloating is down, more energy, sleep better, weight control easier to maintain, not to mention the effect all of these have on diabetes and blood pressure in the long run. I would condone gluten-free products because of the health benefits but on the other hand I have yet to find a gluten-free bread that is palatable to me. So unless you have celiac disease diagnosed by a medical practitioner, go ahead and enjoy fresh foods containing gluten such as plain European style bread with NO additives but keep reading those labels and abstaining from processed foods.

Spices and Rub Mixes

Herbes de Provence

    1 tablespoon dried basil

    1 tablespoon rosemary

    ½ teaspoon sage

    1 teaspoon fennel seeds

    3 tablespoons thyme

    3 tablespoons oregano

    3 tablespoons lavender flowers

    3 tablespoons savory

Mix Well

Five Spice

    3 tablespoons powdered anise

    2 tablespoons black pepper

    1 tablespoon cinnamon

    ½ teaspoon cloves

    4 star anise whole

Process All

Four Spice

1 tablespoon white pepper

2 teaspoons cloves powder

2 teaspoons ground nutmeg

1 teaspoon ground ginger

Mix Well

Dry Rub for Chicken or Pork

¼ cup brown sugar

2 tablespoons Hungarian paprika

2 teaspoons sea salt

1 teaspoon black pepper

1 teaspoon garlic powder (not garlic salt)

1 teaspoon sage powder

1 teaspoon onion powder

½ teaspoon ginger powder

Mix Well.
Great to keep on hand for Barbecuing pork, chicken or beef.

Marinade for Pork Ribs

This marinade is also well suited for Barbequed Chicken or Beef.

½ cup honey

1 cup ketchup

½ cup soya sauce

2 tablespoons crushed garlic

3 tablespoons fresh ginger chopped fine

1 cup sweet chili sauce

½ cup rice vinegar

1 teaspoon five spice mix

Allow for the meat to be in the marinade for at least 1 hour, or better overnight in the fridge.

Place Setting

My good friend, Brian, was over for dinner one night when we started to talk about "this generation" and how it lacks "Savoir faire" when it comes to proper etiquette when dining. After a little research I realized that he had a very valid point, there seems to be a general lack of understanding on the proper way to set a table when entertaining.

When entertaining a dinner party, think of your table as a canvas for your food to be placed on, after all we all know that "eye appeal" in food is primary. An elegant table setting will impress your guests and compliment the taste anticipation of what the food will taste like.

The diagram below is a setting for a very formal dinner, you can customize it to your needs. If you are serving only one type of wine, there is no need for three glasses, and so on!

1. Napkin
2. Salad fork
3. Dinner fork
4. Dessert fork & spoon
5. Bread and butter plate with spreader
6. Dinner plate
7. Dinner knife
8. Teaspoon
9. Soup spoon
10. Cocktail fork
11. Water glass
12. Wine glass (red wine)
13. Wine glass (white wine)
14. Coffee cup and saucer

About the Author

Michel Rabu has being cooking since he was a young teen after the second world war. Born in Brittany, France, Michel has always being exposed to fresh farm food and taught to gather from the wild as much as possible, while his passion for fresh seafood comes from those past experiences. Although his parents where both hairstylists, and aware of European traditions that dictated children (especially boys) were to follow in the family footsteps when it came to profession, Michel worked as a successful hairstylist with International recognition for fifteen years before realizing his true passion was cooking. Having cooked for friends most weekends all of his life, they encouraged him to pursue his dream of opening a restaurant.

His father, Marcel, shared the same passion for cooking, and so they joined forces and opened "The Gourmet by the Sea" restaurant on Vancouver Island. The success was immediate and continued for thirty years. International awards and visits from Hollywood stars and heads of state alike all made "The Gourmet" famous.

CPSIA information can be obtained
at www.ICGtesting.com
Printed in the USA
LVHW07s2043120718
583466LV00003B/9/P

9 781460 263495